Hearts, Minds, Bottom Lines
Investing in Social Capital

To Mike
With thanks
Richard Thomson
Leo Wood
Freya Mcleod.

Hearts, Minds, Bottom Lines

Investing in Social Capital

Les Wood, Richard Thomson, Fiona McLeod

THE McGRAW-HILL COMPANIES

London · Burr Ridge IL · New York · St Louis · San Francisco · Auckland
Bogotá · Caracas · Lisbon · Madrid · Mexico · Milan
Montreal · New Delhi · Panama · Paris · San Juan · São Paulo
Singapore · Sydney · Tokyo · Toronto

 Published by McGraw-Hill Professional
Shoppenhangers Road
Maidenhead
Berkshire
SL6 2QL
Telephone: 44 (0) 1628 502 500
Fax: 44 (0) 1628 770 224
Website: www.mcgraw-hill.co.uk

British Library Cataloguing in Publication Data
A catalogue record for this book is available from the British Library

ISBN: 0 07 709868 4

Library of Congress Cataloguing in Publication Data
The Library of Congress data for this book has been applied for
from the Library of Congress

Sponsoring Editor: Elizabeth Robinson
Editorial Assistant: Sarah Wilks
Business Marketing Manager: Elizabeth McKeever
Senior Production Manager: Max Elvey

Produced for McGraw-Hill by Steven Gardiner Ltd
Text design by Steven Gardiner Ltd
Printed and bound in Great Britain by Bell and Bain Ltd, Glasgow
Cover design by Cinque

McGraw-Hill books are available at special quantity discounts. Please
contact the Corporate Sales Executive at the above address.

Contents

Preface   vii

1   Investing in social capital   1
      Why invest in social capital: the arguments   1
      The shape and flow of the book   7
      Describing the levels in organizations   7
      Defining community   10
      The community elements of social capital   12
      Building community: why try?   27

2   Key interactions   31
      The need to belong to a community of interest   34
      The pursuit of self-interest   36
      Tackling the mix to deliver healthy social capital   37
      The Key Interactions process   41
      The process in detail for facilitators   51

3   Inspiration and strategy   57
      From Vision to reality   58
      The Navigator and the Flight Crew   59
      The Core managers and Activators   60
      Planning to Win   61
      The process stage by stage   65

4   Of hearts and minds and associated body parts   79
      The cast of players   82
      The role of Core manager   82
      A way forward   90
      Engaging Core managers in social capital   93
      A final note   107

5   Delivering the goods   111
      A way forward – or not   114
      The principal features of the programme   117
      The detail of the programme   124
      Overview   132

6   **Tapping the geyser**   133
     The role of coach in developing social capital   135
     The role of facilitator in developing social capital   139
     Contracting for better ways of working   142
     Negociating market deals   151
     Confronting and conflict handling   156
     Learning sets   159

7   **And now for something completely different**   165
     The way forward   171
     Creativity and innovation at work   171
     Involving others and gaining acceptance for new ideas   177
     The Uccello^{TM} Process   178

8   **A glance down some other interesting avenues and a
     pocket summary**   185
     Some other interesting avenues   186
     A pocket summary   190

9   **A tactical guide to investing in social capital**   193

References   197

Index   199

Preface

This book came about in the following way. We had been working as consultants for the last fifteen years – quite successfully really. We had lots of long-term clients, some very effective processes we had developed, a National Training Award in partnership with a well-known multinational and so on.

Clients were saying that we really made a difference but over the last couple of years we began to feel that we could do more. What was needed was an overarching philosophy which would pull everything we do into a coherent and integrated whole. We were pretty sure we had one. There was just so little time to sit down and make it explicit!

So twelve months ago we made the time. The result is what follows. Some of the philosophy is our own, some we thought was our own until we read that others were thinking the same things and some significant insights into connections came from reading people like Francis Fukuyama and James S. Coleman. Some of the processes and mechanisms had their genesis way back in articles read over the decades and have then evolved as a result of working with clients. Others have been created in response to a need and then applied.

We envisage this as a book that readers find easy to use, whether they are reading from the perspective of chief executive, manager, consultant, student or whatever. Readers can either select one or two of the initiatives or adopt the whole as an organization-wide change programme. The latter strategy, we have to admit, would be a first, as mostly we are brought into organizations who have some of the elements either already in place or in the process of being introduced, but the parts all work and they combine well so there is no reason why the sum of the parts should not make a dramatically effective whole.

Whatever you choose, we hope you find it useful.

Chapter 1

Investing in social capital

Capital = something which accrues value, an investment for the future, an appreciating asset, any advantage used as a means of gaining further advantage

Social = pertaining to life in an organized community, pertaining to welfare in such, growing or living in communities, the interaction of people as individuals and groups large and small

Social Capital = the shared norms of behaviour that allow effective co-operation

Why invest in social capital: the arguments

This book provides a practical, integrated approach to achieving and maintaining excellent business performance. It is founded on extensive experience across a wide spectrum of organizations over the last two decades and driven by the following contentions:

- that, in order to be able to achieve, sustain and consistently improve on excellent performance, any modern organization must work in ways which resonate with the fundamental nature and demands of humanity – in other words it must have healthy social capital.
- that society at large is undergoing a major transition, during which

time its ability to meet the full range of human needs is much reduced, particularly in respect of a real sense of community.

• that there is, as a result, a temporary window of opportunity for certain organizations who choose, to seize major advantage by creating climates which are more efficient, more productive, more cost-effective, more profitable and fundamentally more satisfying places to work.

The humanity argument

There are powerful drives, founded in our evolutionary history, both for belonging within a community and for the pursuit of self-interest. There are also strong intellectual and empirical arguments for the effectiveness of collective co-operation to set against the obvious benefits deriving from the pursuit of personal success and recognition. Over the millennia of its existence, homo sapiens has found ways to live and work productively with these opposing drives – at least for appreciable chunks of time. Because of this, we believe that it is possible to view the health of a modern organization's social capital in terms of the degree to which community and self-interest needs are met within its borders.

The problem at present is that many organizations, simultaneously mirroring and influencing society as they do, are failing to provide sufficient opportunities for the satisfaction of their people's community needs. Self-interest is alive and well meanwhile.

The challenge is for organizations to create conditions where these opposing drives can flourish in appropriate proportions. The aim is to achieve excellent performance and bottom line business goals efficiently and effectively through a process of recognizing and meeting some basic human needs. Neither a nice warm comfortable bath of an organization nor a free-for-all gladiatorial contest, but something which more accurately reflects the energy and contradictions of our humanness. Our purpose in this book is to offer a way of creating such a climate, where a healthy social capital makes people feel good about themselves, others and the tasks they perform – where trust is the lubricant and excellent performance is the common obsession.

We have examined what we consider to be the active ingredients necessary for the 'belonging' part of social capital to take its rightful place. It is true that some of these stem from a community past which is now long gone and which may even be of questionable relevance to our new world. However, if the need for them continues to exist in the human psyche, and it really doesn't matter *why* they do so (hard-wired into our psychology or the result of past societal conditioning), then for all practical purposes, today's leaders have little choice but to work with them if they aspire to excellence.

Our arguments are covered in more detail later (see p. 4), but the fact is that most people seem to perform best (i.e. work more efficiently, need less controls, feel more positive and consistently produce better results) when they feel they are part of a community as well as having their self-interest satisfied. Our conclusion is that we can either try to find a way to incorporate these ingredients into our organizations or accept sub-optimal levels of performance achieved only through expensive monitoring and controls. Not surprisingly, we have opted for the former.

The main ingredients from our community past which we have identified as still active and relevant are:

- a sense of belonging and commitment to the greater good;
- reliability, transparency and trust;
- altruism, reciprocity and market deals;
- reputation and self-image;
- competition and co-operation;
- self-interest and the need to belong.

And yet, powerful as they are, these are not in themselves enough. They come from a past which was by no means stable or perfect, but a past where generally there was more time, where most events moved at a slower pace, relationships had longer to mature and change was for the most part gradual, often verging on the imperceptible.

It would be futile to suggest that organizations should attempt to return to conditions of greater stability. Such a move would be impossible right now, even if it were desirable. Conditions have changed, and with them, at least some of the ways of working which bring success. The modern environment is complex and highly interdependent, and sustained success for most is only possible if the interactions between key individuals and groups are of a high quality. To meet these demands and to complete the recipe necessary to form a new healthier social capital, fit for the modern organization, additional ingredients are called for. These are:

- modern heroes;
- risk taking, creativity and innovation;
- a new form of loyalty.

Quite a challenge! However, those organizations that can find a way to offer a strong sense of community in the absence of high levels of stability, have much to gain; not just in current bottom line performance but in future triumphs and expansion.

The temporary window argument

Leaders with the vision and courage to accept the challenge, now find themselves with what may be a 'once in a lifetime' opportunity to seize a critical advantage for the organizations they lead and make life seriously difficult for any competition at the same time, if that too holds a certain appeal. Why now? Because society is going through rapid and major changes, not least amongst which is a significant reduction in the opportunities for people to function effectively within a community. In time it is likely that people will find ways to fill this temporary gap in their lives of their own accord, but for now the opportunity is clear. Smart, winning organizations, as they always do, will identify the need and create satisfying working climates. As a result they will triumph over their competition, whatever form that takes.

If that doesn't sound an exciting prospect, then it would probably be best if you put this book back where you found it. If, however, your organization possesses someone at the top with vision, energy and courage, then read on. If that happens to be you, even better. You may not agree with all we have to say or all the solutions we have to offer. That does not matter. The cardinal sin now is to pretend that everything is more or less alright and that it can be sorted by a bit more training or a bit of restructuring or whatever. This is a time to think and act radical! The choice is to lead now or to follow others later. Those that choose the former will be the excellent performers of the future.

There is a gap in the market. What is missing is enough places for people to work which are rich in healthy social capital. While there may exist some robust and solitary exceptions, most people have a powerful need to belong to, and to identify with, some group or community of interest – usually several. They need some way of knowing where they stand in the community, some rules about how they are expected to work with others and how they in turn can expect to be treated. Certainly, such devices as company value statements and appraisal systems have a role to play, but it is not the major one. Mostly people know these for what they are – well-intentioned words which unfortunately have little bearing on day-to-day reality. Social capital, on the other hand, is about the *existence* of norms, values and obligations, and how these translate into daily behaviour, interactions with key others and ultimately, performance. People know they are real because they actually experience them.

A working environment rich in healthy social capital not only offers the chance of satisfying the need to feel part of something, it also provides people with a means of assessing their worth. It encourages a sense of responsibility and commitment to the whole and even rewards those who work effectively with others in more tangible ways. These things are psychologically satisfying.

There is plenty of evidence to suggest that wider society, in the West at least, is currently failing to meet people's needs in this respect. There are just less and less places people can go where they can feel they belong. Frequently, in the past, people might have had several, reflecting the different aspects of their lives. Family, including relatives up to three generations, in-laws and various adopted aunts and uncles was one such community for much of man's evolution. However, starting with the Industrial Revolution and increasing in pace over the decades until the headlong dash of the last 10–15 years, we have seen a dramatic increase in the speed at which this once basic institution is disintegrating. The statistics on the percentage of people living on their own in many western countries are staggering in their size and implications for society at large.

Looking beyond the family, there were villages, small towns and quarters of larger cities, all of which once lent themselves to the development and maintenance of communities. These too have changed in the face of two world wars, increased opportunities for mobility, technological advances and a veritable tidal wave of rapidly introduced novelty. The result is that the nature, frequency and quality of contacts and interactions within these units has altered significantly. Arguably most have largely ceased to be communities in the traditional sense, instead, evoking in our minds little more than real estate and places to commute from. Others have become something else again, but few now offer the benefits of community that we need.

Of course, while change is constant, it is neither uniform nor unidirectional, and even now we may be seeing the start of a reversal of this trend, facilitated rather paradoxically by some of these same novelties. IT for example may well have some positive contributions to make alongside its potential dangers. However, if such a reversal is really beginning to take place, it will still take some time to have any major effect. In the meantime, our current reality and the reality that organizations will have to work with for the immediate future, is a much more fluid and dynamic thing where opportunities to belong are significantly less than we are used to.

On p. 2, we have suggested that most organizations both reflect and influence trends in the wider society in which they operate, so naturally here too things have changed. Where there was previously at least the illusion of a job for life, and hence a very real kind of community, there is now no such surety. Sudden redundancy, mergers and takeovers, changes in chief executives, competition, foreign investment priorities, privatization, new technology and other factors, have all combined to render job security and stability a much rarer thing than it was. We have more short-term contracts and high volatility, greater loyalty to professions than to companies, more self-interest and less real teamwork. It is now difficult to find one organizational variable which is not either already experiencing change or appears liable to do so at any moment, and worst of all for our sense of community, the people keep changing as well. Even the information revolution has been a mixed blessing in the respect that it offers the temptation for less face-to-face communication – not necessarily a good thing for social animals like ourselves. The social capital of organizations is depleted and most people don't like it. Smart, winning organizations will find clever ways to fill the gap currently left by society, and, by providing an attractive climate, will secure a competitive advantage before society finds its own solutions.

The pay-off argument

Primarily, organizations which decide to buck the societal trend and provide more rounded, psychologically satisfying environments to work in, will get better performance, produced more economically as a return on their investment. This will be brought about by, amongst other things, people giving more of themselves, taking more risks, and contributing ideas to the community which they are currently keeping to themselves against the prospect of future personal gain. Because these will be more satisfying places to work they will attract better people who will stay as long as they are needed. With better people they will run more efficiently and will need less controls. Consistently better results will generate even more positive feelings about the organization. They will become places which are strong in the qualities people need to be able to feel good about themselves, others and the tasks they perform.

People will still show a healthy self-interest of course. That drive is also built in. The difference is that self-interest is currently alive and well and living happily within western organizations – by invitation! It needs no more encouragement than it is already getting at present. At least no more of the kind it has been getting. However, we believe that there are ways to encourage individual achievement which actually contribute to the stock of healthy social capital and these are incorporated into the processes and tools we offer throughout the book.

Our offer

This book is about changing the way organizations work internally and how they interact with the people who are not part of the organization but who are key to its success and survival. It is about customers, suppliers, employees and managers all of whom we have assumed to be more or less human. It is about creating a new deal between them, one which resonates more harmoniously with our humanity.

Naturally, everyone reading this book will have a view about how well their organization is doing in this respect. We know there must be some who are making it work really well, although we often find that rosy perspective thriving better in the boardroom than on the shop floor. Most organizations will be doing some of the things we suggest and a few will wonder which planetary system we hail from. For the last of these, let us assure you that the air is breathable and the life forms are both entertaining and dangerous. In any case we hope we have added something to the debate.

The shape and flow of the book

The book is structured as follows:

Chapter 1 caters for those readers who would like a reasonably quick overview of the background arguments before getting into the practical detail of each chapter. There is an explanation of the terminology we have had to develop for the organizational levels we talk about, and there is a health checklist on pp. 29–30.

Chapters 2–7 contain the processes which can be used to deliver or speed up your organization's progress toward healthier social capital. In each of these six chapters we offer:

- analyses and arguments for our recommended approach;
- checklists so that you can assess your organization against the key messages offered and its state of readiness for action;
- some guidance notes on how to make the particular process work.

Lastly, the final chapter brings together the material into a pocket summary in addition to touching on some non-behavioural options for assisting the journey towards healthier social capital. At the end there is a tactical guide to help you position each of the initiatives in relation to the conditions which currently prevail in your organization.

We have tried to make the whole book like a house with many entrances so that you can easily find those parts that are of immediate interest and relevance to you and your organization. The checklists are there to help you decide whether your organization would benefit from applying the processes, either singly or as part of a whole integrated change strategy.

For those whom the reference to 'applying the processes' has just cheered enormously and who are itching to get into the 'doing' chapters and the checklists, we may be about to say *au revoir*. Please come back and visit when you are ready. You may need the background that this chapter contains to convince some of your key others. However, just before you go, you may find the next two sections useful in your reading of the rest of the book, as they provide a couple of key definitions – the first being the terms we use to describe the general levels in organizations and the second, the concept of community in this context.

Describing the levels in organizations

Every organization has titles for their people, the roles they fulfil and the positions they hold. Writing this book presented a problem that was new for us. We needed to find and use some which were general enough to encompass the different but broadly synonymous titles employed by organizations but also added something to the reader's understanding. We wanted to avoid tricky and quirky titles, and to find some which at least nodded in the direction of reflecting what people at each of the levels do – an 'It does what it says on the can' philosophy, if you like. Whether we have succeeded or not you can judge.

For the purposes of this book, and in a necessarily coarse overview of organization structures in general, we propose four levels where leadership and management behaviours figure significantly:

1 the leader;
2 senior managers;
3 middle managers; and
4 first-line managers plus a few others who are either in non-managerial but central positions and/or who are opinion formers.

Each will have different but explicit and valued contributions to make, delivered via a unique mix of behaviours – some leadership, some managerial.

As the book grew we found that none of the above titles met our criteria. They were just too much in common use and had too many different meanings and interpretations. They seemed more likely to confuse than illuminate. So we developed the following titles which we employ throughout the book. The intention is that they should be descriptive and not in any way confining or restricting, so we do not suggest looking for the perfect match in your own organization. Instead they should be viewed as broad categories within which there is some commonality of role. We hope they work for you. They are Navigator, Flight Crew, Core and Activators.

The *Navigator* is the person at the top. After considering some more exotic titles we decided we liked it best because it says something about looking up and out, seeing ahead and showing the way. We even tried Pilogator which was an unhappy marriage of Pilot and Navigator but felt that was taking things a bit too far.

The Navigator is the one with the organization-wide vision. S/he is the unifying figure, who carries the responsibility for ensuring that the Flight Crew (the senior managers) understand and buy into the vision and their role in its realization. The Navigator's job is to create momentum through personal drive and energy, to be high profile, to be outrageous from time to time and to inspire. They will also spread the word on the strategy for delivering the vision and constantly reinforce 'good' behaviours in the wider organization.

All this may leave little time and energy for managerial behaviours such as coaching and facilitating, which are so essential to the development of healthy social capital. In the Navigator's case, however, this is not always a bad thing. There are few people who are able to excel in all aspects of leadership and management and some Navigators, while extremely talented at what they do, should definitely be kept away from the latter. In these circumstances, perhaps we should applaud them for the strengths and talents they bring, and not trouble them too much for the ones they haven't got.

The *Flight Crew* are the senior managers. They are the champions, the disciples, the executives of the developing strategy. They are strategic thinkers of some note and visionaries in their own right, albeit that their visions must serve the overall. They are the ones who ensure the integration and timing of developments into a coherent whole across the organization.

Their role is to drive the translation of the organization-wide vision into practical reality. They will work hard to communicate and inspire everyone to give their all, both to that vision and the numerous supporting visions it spawns. They will be articulate and inspirational, energetic and brimming with infectious commitment. If they are not, why should anyone follow?

In some senses their job is tougher than the Navigator's, for whom the mix of leadership and managerial behaviours can be heavily weighted towards the former. For the Flight Crew to be effective, their mix must contain significant elements of both. They must be able to create coherent and co-ordinated strategic momentum, and for this, they will require to exhibit large amounts of self-discipline and good judgement. They must be able to take the Navigator's 'light-bulb' ideas, and anyone else's for that matter, and decide which ones to light, and, more importantly, which ones not to. Many are the organizations that have lost their way on the trail of too many initiatives. The Flight Crew's role here is to select only the most productive ones, concentrate the organization's resources on what will deliver the goods, and develop some consistency of policy and approach. At the same time they must be alert and responsive to any important changes and opportunities – flexible consistency in fact! No wonder the job is so difficult!

They must be able to plan effectively. They must produce strategies which are well thought through, so that plans are based on solid foundations and not subject to sudden arbitrary changes in direction. They must be analytical and focused, always on the alert for upcoming changes in law, market, technology and the rest, which will affect the potential the organization has for success in the future, as well as its immediate ability to compete wherever it needs to.

Like the Navigator, they must be constant role models, but in some respects their impact on the culture of the organization can be even greater. While the Navigator sets the tone, it is the Flight Crew who are better equipped to spread it. There are enough of them to reach out and touch all parts of the organization, and the managerial aspects of their roles will usually bring them into more frequent contact with large numbers of its people. Coaching and mentoring, for example, might take only a small proportion of their time, but can offer an opportunity to exert a major influence on the behaviour of key players. The frequency and nature of more general daily contacts also offers the Flight Crew the prospect of developing positive reputations, with the implicit or explicit invitation to those who work for them, to emulate their behaviour in return for enjoying the political and tactical benefits of working for a boss with clout and credibility.

The *Core* of most organizations is represented by the middle managers. We are somewhat concerned that the role of manager may have become devalued in recent years, in favour of the often inaccurate, but apparently more fashionable, title of leader. In later chapters we look in some detail at the power of this group to bring about healthier social capital, so we will not spend a lot of time on them here. Suffice it to say that we believe the Core to be the single most powerful group in influencing the practical adoption of organizational change. They can engage those who work for them, act as both a filter and a conduit for the ideas passing up and down, and, using coaching and facilitating skills, grow their people's abilities to deliver in an environment of improving social capital. To do this they must relinquish much of the hands-on control they may have grown comfortable with and replace it with influence.

Their central position in the organization, their power to influence those who work for them and their knowledge and experience, makes them seriously heavy hitters in this context. So often perceived as barriers to new ways, in fact they can be major assets – always provided they see that it is in their interests to be so.

The *Activators* are the first-line managers and other, often non-managerial, players who are in positions of some influence. They too have a chapter to themselves, so we will be very brief. In essence they are the people who organize the resources at the operational level and deliver the goods. They make the ideas work. They build on them. When they are engaged and feel a real sense of belonging they make the minor adjustments to ideas, systems and processes that are needed to really make them work in practice.

In summary, the mix of leadership and managerial behaviours appropriate to each job is as varied as the jobs themselves (see Table 1.1).

Defining community

In seeking a definition for 'community' in this context, we have looked to collective behaviour – to the way individuals and groups perceive and interact with each other. Our contention is that if people as a matter of

Table 1.1

Our title	Who they might be	What they do (in brief)
Navigator	Chief executive, managing director, president, owner	Show the way and chart the course. Produce the vision for the organization as a whole. Keep the Flight Crew on track and unified. Create momentum and inspire across the whole organization. Constantly reinforce 'good' behaviours.
The Flight Crew	Board of directors, senior managers	Drive the translation of the organization-wide vision towards its realization, creating their own supporting visions on the way. Act as champions, disciples and executives. Inspire, create coherent and co-ordinated strategic momentum.
The Core	Middle managers	Link the strategic momentum to the operational, just like putting an engine into gear. Create the environment where people grow and are prepared to give more of themselves in exchange for belonging. Use influence rather than control.
The Activators	First-line managers, and other often non-managerial players who are in positions of some influence.	Deliver the goods. Manage and lead day-to-day activities. Act in ways which reinforce the drive towards healthier social capital.

course exhibit behaviours which convey attitudes such as respect, trust, reliability and so on, then the collective experience is likely to be a psychologically satisfying one and a sense of belonging and community can be said to exist. There is a problem of course about what to do when these are not present or are insufficiently represented and also about how to keep them once you have them. It is on concerns such as these that this book is focused.

The community elements of social capital

The ingredients which organizations must actively manage for the community element of social capital to take its rightful station, relative to the pursuit of self-interest, are:

A sense of belonging and commitment to the greater good

Commonly, today's working environment gives little encouragement to people to really feel part of the whole operation and this at a time when organizations need to ask more and more from their human resource in order to stay ahead of the game. Good words abound in the shape of vision, mission and value statements but on the whole, people know what is really going on from the way they are treated, and what they know often tells them to hold something back. As a result, they contribute less overall than they could. They take fewer risks. They tell less than they know. They look after their own interests at the expense of others. The wisdom of such a stance is often reinforced by a number of other powerful influencers ranging from the often divisive day-to-day behaviour of senior managers (Flight Crew) through to pay and benefits policies which support the pursuit of self-interest to the detriment, even the exclusion of collective achievement.

Another factor which militates against the existence of a sense of community and makes it so apparently unfashionable just now is that there is a price to be paid for belonging, a membership fee if you like. Why? Because, by definition, each individual's needs and desires are almost inevitably going to be slightly different and sometimes even at odds with the other members of any community of interest whether it is the Auchtermuchty Pig Fanciers or a department within a prestigious multinational. In order to move forward as a reasonably harmonious and co-ordinated body into a bright and in a relatively few cases, porcine future, there must be some give and take, some understanding and generosity. Equally there must be some valued benefit to compensate for the loss of maximization of individual fulfilment.

Look around your place of work. How long have you worked there? How long will you stay? Who has been there the longest, and how many have been around for less than two years? How committed do you feel to them – not to the unit or department goals – but to them? You may have some values which will make it difficult to answer this question without discomfort but give it a try. How prepared are you to sacrifice an important personal success for the greater good, for the organizational commonwealth? How typical is that attitude?

The challenge for today's ambitious organizations is to create a working environment where people demonstrate their willingness on a daily basis to commit and contribute all they are capable of to the greater good, in exchange for a feeling that they belong – that they are a part of something they value. As an added bonus for such organizations, if one is required, managers at all levels will also be freed up to concentrate much more on delivering output appropriate to their talents and salaries.

Reliability, transparency and trust

Francis Fukuyama, in his book *Trust – The Social Virtues and Creation of Prosperity*, suggests that 'Trust is the expectation that arises within a community of regular, honest and co-operative behaviour.' This would seem to suggest it is more a product of experience than a given. If so, then it has to be earned and that takes time.

In the small, relatively stable communities of the past, people had a good idea what to expect from others. They could rely on people to behave more or less consistently over time, not least because there was time. This allowed them to become three-dimensional for each other. By that we mean that they had the opportunity to see each other operating in more than one setting, responding to more than one set of stimuli, performing more than one role. They had the opportunity to find out a bit more about the whole person with whom they were dealing, and as a result tolerance, understanding and the desire to co-operate for the greater good could grow. And yes of course, there were feuds and tribalism, wars and petty bickering and malicious gossip and all the other things that human beings like to get up to. But however unattractive these were, at least there was a possibility of their being held in check by the more positive community forces. In many of today's organizations that counterbalance seems woefully weak for the job.

Now, many of the people you have to deal with are strangers and we are not talking about one-off customers or the person in front of you in the Starbucks coffee queue. These are the people you interact with in order to get your daily work done. Working life is fast and demanding. Stability is low and turnover is high. Change is endemic and possibly chronic. There is little time to get to know one another, and mostly there is little real encouragement from organizations either. Some platitudes perhaps, but in practice all the time and space is already used up by work activity. As a result, colleagues, even in the same department, but certainly beyond it, are often little more than recognizable strangers – cardboard cut-outs, two-dimensional beings. This does not make for transparency and trust, and when you think about it, reliability in these conditions is only something you need to show to impress a few people before you move on. More of a tactic than a state of being. How can we trust people we do not know or understand?

One morning a vice-president made the mistake of asking one of his managers how he was. The manager, taking the enquiry at face value, began his answer. But the VP was feeling under some pressure to get on and after a couple of sentences during which he tried some bits of non-verbal communication from his repertoire without much noticeable effect, he cried 'Stop! Look Bill! It was only a figure of speech. Right?' How can we trust people if we don't know them, and how can we know them if we only have time for the task in hand and none for even the most superficial of social niceties?

Recently there have been some suggestions that the long hours cultures which prevail in many organizations are actually giving rise to close circles of friends at work. Could this be a counter argument to the preceding paragraph? We think not. For one thing, there are too many down sides to long hours cultures for us to consider advocating it as a means of delivering *healthy* social capital. For another, our objective is to engage people in delivering excellent performance and there is no guarantee that a community with its genesis in such a culture would see that as its *raison d'être*. Arguably, quite the reverse.

Some see a partial answer in value statements, but in truth they can never be more than that. They may impress outsiders and they can even be used as levers to shed unwanted senior managers (Flight Crew), but as inspirational beacons for the creation of community they leave much to be desired. Training and development initiatives represent another laudable but partial solution, although in many instances they are perceived more as unaffordable luxuries by the hard-pressed participants who have to find time out of their 'real jobs' to take part in them.

In fact the solution has to be much more practically oriented, much more directly connected to real work. What is required is a process which concentrates on improving specific elements of performance without incurring real-time penalties, which enhances ways of working collectively and replicates the behaviours of the community to such an extent that, through repeated successful practice, these behaviours become absorbed into the norms of the organization – because they work and they feel right.

When that happens, organizations will have rediscovered the qualities of community which are now so crucially lacking. Trust becomes possible because people know from experience that they can rely on deals being honoured over time. Understanding is enhanced because in order to do the deal people have had to listen and understand the other person's position. It is the process of doing and honouring a deal, which builds the trust and which lubricates the wheels.

The challenge for leaders is to tackle real behaviours in the workplace and to press through highly visible and transparent mechanical processes, which will give birth to new communities. The opportunity and the pay-off is to help people to become three-dimensional for each other, so that their actions are more understandable, their behaviour is in a real sense more predictable, their word more reliable. In these conditions traditional training and development activities such as team building will again be valid but will be properly a question of refinement. Value statements will be so obvious as to be unworthy of comment from those who already belong except for when they are enthusing about their place of work. Ways of achieving this are described in Chapters 2–7.

Reciprocal altruism and market deals

One of the problems for modern organizations, stemming from people's inability to find enough time to get to know key others well, is that there is now often insufficient data available to be sure that interacting parties are playing the game by the same set of rules. This diminishes a process of 'reciprocal altruism', which has long been part of humanity's way of doing business.

One good turn deserves another, they say. In the close-knit, more stable communities of our past, there was usually ample opportunity to develop complicated unspoken checks and balances which by and large worked to even things out over time, ensuring that some degree of equity applied or was at least perceived amongst the members of the community, or if it did not, that the offending party paid in some other way, however subtle. The phrase used to describe this unspoken process is *reciprocal altruism*. It does best in relatively stable conditions where most apparently altruistic acts can be performed in the knowledge that it is likely that some unspecified and uncontracted benefit will accrue to the perpetrator of that act at some time in the future. This allows interactions between members of the community to be *unspoken, time-shifted and non-specific*.

Like trust however, while it may be *present* as a convention, reciprocal altruism is something which *emerges* as a result of repeat experience. It is likely to thrive in conditions where behaviour, reputation and self-image are closely linked, where relationships are of sufficiently long standing and where there is some degree of confidence (however misplaced) that this will continue long into the future. Stability of community membership, a reasonably consistent and commonly accepted set of rules for how to play the game, and some consensus about what is good and important will also help to create the conditions where people are surer of their worth because that worth can be seen through the eyes of others.

And here is a dilemma. Given that few, if any of these conditions are set to return to modern working life in the near future, leaders (Navigators) must find some other way if they want to secure the organizational benefits that accrue from the widespread application of the process of reciprocal altruism. Because people seem to like it. We cling to it even though the conditions that made it effective in the first place no longer really exist. It feels like the *proper* way to do things. Indeed, any attempt to make a deal explicit may be frowned upon as not good manners and far too calculating. However, our partiality for the process may not be enough to save it. Human beings are creatures with strong self-serving instincts, which will dominate unless effectively countered. A workable alternative is required or rather a means of creating the practice of reciprocal altruism in conditions which do not naturally favour its spontaneous development. Organizations wishing to develop healthy social capital need to find some other method of building up the practice amongst their people. This method, curiously, is through the development of the unspeakable – the habit of market deals!

Ironically, market deals, the method by which reciprocal altruism can once again be installed as a powerful influence in driving excellent performance as well as developing healthier social capital, are *declared, time-present and highly specific*; almost the exact opposite of the condition they seek to bring about.

The market deals method is founded in an experience with which we are all familiar – the process of learning, in which we move from unconscious incompetence, to conscious incompetence, to conscious competence, and lastly to unconscious competence. In order to be able to move from an unsatisfactory situation, where we have insufficient skill or where we are using sub-optimal behaviours or where we need to master a new idea or way of working, it seems we often have to go through a conscious stage when we focus our attention on the mechanics of doing. It is the time when the golf professional gives you the new swing and you have to consciously set yourself up and think about it as you do it. Only after some practice does the new swing groove in, and then the action becomes unconscious. It has then joined your tool kit of skills and you can now swing away on autopilot to mix two metaphors cruelly. This journey through the uncomfortable conscious stages applies just as much to the changes in interactive behaviours we need to develop to allow us eventually to reinstate reciprocal altruism amongst the organizational norms.

We have observed that where reciprocal altruism is unspoken, time-shifted and non-specific, the process of market deals is exactly the opposite. A market deal is explicit, usually spoken, but with the conclusion often recorded on paper or computer. It is a deal done at the time, although it may have stages, milestones and benefits which accrue to different parties at different times. Perhaps that needs more explaining. In reciprocal altruism, one act is not linked to another, while in market deals it is. The process is described more fully in Chapters 2 and 6, but in essence, doing market deals demands that people take time to understand each other's needs and wants in a specific area of work or task, work out together the best ways to interact in order to achieve the best result *for the organization*, agree how each party will act in future (e.g. deliver on time, improve quality of output) and then honour the agreement in practice over time. In so doing relationships are enhanced, there is opportunity to show reliability and long-standing devils are dehorned.

Only when the market deals process reaches the unconscious competence stage will people be able to become less explicit in their deals. At that point, if prevailing conditions ever allow it to be reached, the need for overt and explicit market deals may diminish because it will have been replaced by unspoken, time-shifted and non-specific interactions – by reciprocal altruism in fact! Until then the only route to low maintenance (minimal monitoring and controls) and high performance interactions lies through market deals.

The long-term challenge for Navigators (leaders) is to create and maintain conditions in their organizations where reciprocal altruism is able to prosper. The short-term challenge is to find a way to get there at a time when the conditions are somewhat hostile.

The opportunity and pay-off is that people will again feel that it is worth making sacrifices for the greater good. The result will be an organization with few functional barriers which shares its information and expertise freely and efficiently and which, as a consequence, is robust, self-sustaining and self-improving.

Before going on, you may wish to check out your own organization against some of the conditions described so far – or not, of course.

Checklist

In my organization:

Behaviour, reputation and self-image are closely linked	I Agree/I Disagree
Relationships are of long standing	I Agree/I Disagree
There is confidence and even certainty that this will continue long into the future	I Agree/I Disagree
People sacrifice their own interests for the greater good	I Agree/I Disagree
We do not waste resources on monitoring and controls. We are a low maintenance, high performance organization.	I Agree/I Disagree
People take time to understand each other's point of view.	I Agree/I Disagree
Quality information is shared as readily as it should be with those who need it.	I Agree/I Disagree
There is stability of community membership.	I Agree/I Disagree
The rules of the game are constant and not subject to change.	I Agree/IDisagree
Values about what is good and what is important change only slowly over time.	I Agree/I Disagree
People are sure of their worth and that their worth can be seen through the eyes of others.	I Agree/I Disagree
Reciprocal altruism is evident in people's normal daily behaviour.	I Agree/I Disagree

If you either answered Disagree or perhaps wished there was a 'maybe' category, it is likely that, where high performance is being maintained at present, it is achieved at considerable expense in terms of monitoring and controls and involvement of higher levels of management than should strictly speaking be necessary.

Reputation and self-image

We live in an age of instant reputation. We are fed someone's character in sound bites, or draw some quick and often dirty conclusions ourselves on the basis of one or two actions on the other's part. We do not have time to allow the rounded picture to develop. We must go with what we have, and tailor our treatment of the individual concerned accordingly.

It wasn't always like this. In the small communities of our past, if you got yourself a bad reputation, it had a tendency to stay with you forever. Take the story of the otherwise generous and virtuous villager who, as a result of one, hopefully apocryphal, youthful indiscretion, was known for ever more as 'Baaa–baaa'. Try to tell him that reputation isn't important! More commonly, someone who develops a reputation for honesty in a community can expect to be treated very differently from someone with a questionable reputation in that area. The same is true of temper, reliability, talent, trustworthiness, etc.

Why is reputation, deserved or otherwise, so powerful? One reason is that reputation invites certain behaviours in others. As we have observed, people treat the person with an honest reputation differently than they do the reputedly dishonest one. As the consequences of the latter treatment are self-evidently less favourable, most people try to maintain positive reputations for honesty or the other qualities that are held to be important in the communities of which they are members. Whether this is a conscious or an unconscious process is debatable and not particularly relevant to the practical considerations of this book. Either way, a positive reputation produces a positive response in others and so makes life easier, more pleasant and often more rewarding for the individual concerned, as well as for those with whom they must interact.

In essence the positive opinion of others tends to provoke a repetition of the good behaviours which the community values and acts as a deterrent to bad behaviour, whatever the community might consider that to be. Good and bad in this sense have nothing to do with wider morality but rather are used to indicate approval or otherwise within the community. Hence the good and bad epithets can apply just as easily to organized crime syndicates as to charities like Oxfam and Children in Need or the Red Cross. More practically, good from the community's perspective could be defined as anything which sustains and enriches it over time and that applies to its internal workings as much as to the interactions with key others beyond the community boundary.

The processes which surround reputation have much to do with the well-known principles of positive and negative reinforcement. This relationship also has the effect of *extending* their ability to mould future behaviour, and to reach deep into a person's being to their self-image. It would be going too far to say we are how we are treated, but if we are treated in a particular way by those around us, it can be difficult to resist their collective judgement over long periods of time. The person with a reputation for tight-fistedness may find that any acts of generosity on their part are barely noticed by others who seem blinded by that long held and widespread view. The absence of positive reinforcement would therefore tend to reduce the instances of generosity in all but the most determined individuals. In this way, we can see that reputation can be self-fulfilling and self-sustaining as well as providing an impetus for improving future behaviour; whatever that might mean for a given community.

The same *potential* to influence also exists at the level of organizational behaviour, particularly as many modern organizations take pride in viewing themselves as open systems, aware of and responsive to their environment. However, in practice, the impact of reputation on ways of working, practised value systems (as opposed to declared ones), interactions between people generally and specifically and hence its value as a positive force for excellent performance, has been eroded drastically in recent times.

The sources of this erosion are not hard to find. Geographical and occupational mobility, for example, are on the increase. There can be very few people who expect to stay with their current company for the duration of their working life. Many employees are on short-term contracts, and even those who are not, are unlikely to rule out a significant move in the next 5 years. Constant internal change means people move on or out at an increasing pace. One consequence of this is that there is less perception of the organization as a community and the power of reputation has diminished accordingly or at least altered beyond all recognition. If you develop an unsatisfactory reputation, you can always just leave it behind you by changing careers or employers.

Bearing in mind the tendency of organizations to both reflect and influence societal trends, it would be surprising if we did not see something similar there; and indeed we do! Way back, most people's reputations would have been limited to not much more than those with whom they came into direct contact. As communications improved, so reputations were able to spread without such direct contact, and we now find ourselves in a time when we often know more about prominent people's lives than we know about the person at the next desk. We are used to absorbing the most intimate facts about strangers and drawing conclusions based on the flimsiest of unsubstantiated information about their intellect, their morality, their ability and so on. We have moved away from reputations based on actual behaviour and into the realm of sound-bite reputation. Want to lose a poor reputation? Simply hire a good spin-doctor and make yourself a new one.

Reputation is a basic part of human currency, and, as such, it has the capacity to affect everyone at all levels in an organization. Its current weakened and altered state offers an opportunity for leaders to take action to release its full power as a motivating force within their organizations and so create healthier social capital and sustained excellent performance.

The challenge for leaders (Navigators) is to identify to what extent this fundamental shaper of human behaviour is at work in their organizations today, to create conditions which will allow reputation to revive and thrive as a positive force, to harness this force in the pursuit of the organization's goals and to challenge their own behaviour and resolve to become a highly visible role model for the people of the organization. The opportunity and pay-off is to enhance the productive social capital of the organization and focus its power on the achievement of the organization's goals.

Competition, co-operation, self-interest and the need to belong

We may have a built-in need to belong but we are also quite attracted to the idea of the pursuit of self-interest and winning. As a species we are instinctively inclined to compete and yet this is tempered by a recognition of the benefits of co-operation. We want recognition and respect on an individual basis but we also want the success that increased co-operation brings. It is clear that these two basic impulses make uncomfortable bedfellows. In the development of healthy social capital, it is necessary that both these aspects of human nature are adequately catered for in people's working lives.

Right now, the picture is mixed and while many organizations are *talking* about teams and collective effectiveness, their reward systems still seem for the most part to concentrate on individuals. People are quick to note which behaviour brings home the bacon. The result is that co-operation outside the immediate boundaries of individual units often has to be enforced through complex, cumbersome, bureaucratic or contractual arrangements or encouraged by expensive team building initiatives. Because they are artificial, these 'rules of engagement' must be constantly checked and monitored, diverting expensive managerial effort which could be better employed.

Of course, humankind has proved that it *can* co-operate quite well without much in the way of healthy social capital being present, in particular trust. In its absence, we have laws, rules, legal contracts, binding agreements and the like to ensure that co-operation takes place with some degree of regularity. These arrangements have stood the test of time and will no doubt continue to do so. However, while such forms of co-operation work, they are not necessarily the most efficient way of interacting. Contracts have to be drawn up carefully in case some unwitting advantage is given to the other party. Changes to these contracts must also be subject to the same rigorous examination. These things take time. They require expensive specialist expertise. Advantage can be lost while these mechanisms grind along. Nonetheless it is beyond doubt that this mechanistic process of co-operation represents a necessary caution in the wider society. Where it should be inappropriate but is currently, necessarily and wastefully in common use is *within* many organizations.

Inside an organization there is, in theory at least, a commonality of purpose. There is, or should be, an implicit and obvious benefit to co-operation. There should be an understanding of commonwealth, of destinies bound together in the performance of the company. There should be an understanding too of the differentiated activities and how these separate contributions combine to achieve the greater good. In these circumstances we should be entitled to expect that a co-operative, community environment will work more efficiently than one which must be constantly policed. Where healthy social capital has been developed, trust, or something that acts just like it, offers even more benefits, such as an increased ability to respond quickly to new events and to allow new arrangements to be put in place without the slowing drag of time and cost expensive contractual negotiations.

On the basis of these arguments alone, it would make sense for any organization that can, to seize the opportunity of developing a healthier social capital. Yet there is an even stronger argument. The organizations which do so, will be offering their people an experience which is much more satisfying than the mechanistic, monitored and controlled alternative. They will be offering a working experience which resonates with some of the fundamental aspects of what it means to be human. In so doing, they will be acquiring the passionate commitment of their people, and the word will spread, the best people will be attracted and will stay. All that is required is for an organization to create the necessary work environment; one where people have a process to work out for themselves the best solution for their commonwealth, one where trust can be developed over time, one which encourages co-operation while recognizing the desire for individual or partisan achievement, one which is much more self-managing than managed.

The process we offer produces the same effects as trust. In a sense it is a mechanical process which requires people to adopt the dance steps first. If the music comes along later and trust develops, then that is a bonus. The main objective is to develop the habits of trust to counteract the competitive instincts which currently hold sway.

The challenge is to create a whole workforce which is tuned into the organization's goals, where differentiated activities and individual contributions are naturally integrated by effective daily interactions, thus allowing fast action, economic internal processes, quick responses and far-sightedness. The opportunity and pay-off is to draw the benefits from a climate in which the big picture is widely understood and everyone works towards it without regard to parochial advantage and with an eye constantly on excellent performance.

The need for heroic leaders and our current aversion to them

Do we still look up to our leaders any more? We tolerate them certainly, avoid them and even spend a bit of time trying to hoodwink them. We know their failings better than we admit their strengths. Is this cynicism or just the natural response of a sophisticated and better educated society? It kind of begs the question as to whether we even still have leaders worthy of the name, and of course, are we prepared to accept a genuine one when they come along?

We certainly have people who *call* themselves leaders. The title is everywhere. Some organizations seem to have nothing but! The intent is understandable, but if these new leaders only spend a tiny proportion of their time actually leading and the rest really managing, what price the currency? And what about these 'leaders' themselves? Is it out of embarrassment at the erroneous title that they have learned to be cautious and democratic and politically correct? The trouble is that in difficult times, and these certainly seem to *be* difficult times, might that not be just when a real leader or two would come in handy?

And so to heroes – anachronisms or lost saviours? Can leaders still be heroes, even part of the time? It is axiomatic that few people, if any, are capable of being heroes across the whole of their activities or for long periods of time. In one way this is a bit sad, because sometimes it might be comforting to believe that there are a significant number of people who are bigger, better, more honest, braver yet kinder, wiser yet not inclined to take advantage of their wisdom to the detriment of others and so on. But if our brave new world has shown us anything, it has shown us that the vast majority, if not all the heroes of the past, were not giants who lived lives which we could only admire but instead, rather ordinary people who, in one brief moment or in one specific aspect of their lives, acted heroically. And yet therein lies something positive. If true, then surely it rather opens up the hero game to, well, everyone really!

When we think of what a heroic leader should be, what do we envisage? Some sacrifice (time, energy, personal security, etc.) perhaps, that goes beyond a rational calculation of potential personal gain. Some action that inspires the rest of us to try harder to be better people, achieve more or try something that would otherwise be out of the question. Some excitement. When they are on a roll, heroes should set us on fire and make us excel. Good Heavens, can this still be organizations we are talking about? Why not? Even in our cynical times, where with enough digging, everyone can be shown to have feet of clay, and there is an unhealthy and macabre desire to expose the weaknesses of everyone, no matter how great they seem, aren't most of us still secretly thrilled by the prospect of a genuine hero?

So what has gone wrong? Where are they? Have *we* changed or do we just find ourselves in a period of history where the leadership assembly line is having a few quality control problems? If so, the timing is particularly poor. We are in the midst of a period of dramatic and fundamental change. We need leaders now who lead; people who stand up and inspire others to try harder, to be more altruistic and to take more risks. We need true Leviathans. Yet, for the most part, leadership in industry seems to have become unfashionable.

Leaders have become coy about their role. Is it quite the done thing for a leader to have a vision which they passionately believe in and which they pursue with single-minded energy and dedication? It almost seems that we are not sure if this would be seen as entirely acceptable behaviour. When the company vision and mission are developed over several meetings by the chief executive and the board of directors, the result may be correct and even well written, but it is not stirring. It may be more democratic, but does it still inspire? Surely people *want* to be led by someone who believes passionately in what they are doing, who gets it wrong because they try too hard or feel the passion too much, whose descriptions about their visions are not necessarily well constructed but a bit rough and ready, whose energy overrides any flaws in their syntax and allows us to forgive the inadvertent politically incorrect behaviour or the poor coaching skills. It may be time to ask our heroes back, and, if so, we may need to accept that they are not perfect and can be a bit rough around the edges.

On the other hand, maybe *we* are the problem; maybe we are getting the leaders we deserve. Are we still ready to be inspired and thrilled by our leaders? Perhaps we are suspicious of being stirred by our jobs. Perhaps it is more cool to stand back emotionally from the company for which we work. Then we can always disown it when things don't work out. 'It wasn't *our* personal vision. *We* don't feel any personal loss or responsibility. It was *the company*. Oh well, time to move on and look for another job.' If we want heroic leaders, we may have to take a look at ourselves as well.

The challenge is to give back to leaders the license to lead. More than that, perhaps it is time we demanded it. The good news is that leadership and heroism, whilst essential requirements for those at the top, are definitely a game all the family can play.

Whilst the Navigator (chief executive, etc.) and the Flight Crew (senior managers) should by rights spend most of their time and energy in leading, leadership behaviour can be anywhere in the organization. What is important is not to confuse it with managerial behaviour, which is just as important but very different (see Chapters 3, 4 and 6). By recognizing this distinction as proper, we can actually free up both functions to contribute their full potential to the development of healthier and enhanced performance.

Risk-taking, creativity and innovation

Many organizations currently stifle creativity, innovation and risk taking while often, at the same time, declaring that they are champions of all three. This is the difference between declared policy and actual policy – what people say they do and what they can actually be seen doing. It is one of the things that causes many employees below board level to laugh hollowly – but discreetly – at the grand pronouncements contained in value statements, mission statements and the like. Risk taking, creativity and innovation are fundamental human drives, but so is the instinct for survival and no amount of fine words will convince someone, who has just seen a colleague take it on the chin for adopting one or more of the above trinity, to have a go themselves.

Risk comes in many forms, of course, that associated with creativity and innovation being just one amongst many. We can take a risk with our reputation, our credibility, our future, our money, our lives, our trust. Some risks may critically affect our future well-being and some may be minor. Some risk taking by its people may be essential to one organization, whereas another may get along relatively well for long periods without it. What represents a risk is also a very personal judgement, with one person's scary risk being another's exciting stimulation.

In this book, we will be focusing particularly on risk taking in the areas of creativity and innovation first because these activities are so relevant to the potential success of many of today's organizations but also because appropriate risk taking in any field of activity or behaviour is an essential component of healthy social capital.

Something has gone wrong with the deal that organizations are offering when it comes to risk taking. Or maybe there never was a good understanding of what made it a worthwhile pastime. What *is* certain is that organizations now need their people to understand what beneficial risk-taking means and particularly how it really links with creativity and innova-tion. Currently a lot of the words sound right, but the deeds fall short. Too often, the workforce understand all too clearly that the kind of risks the organization likes, are those that pay off. Risks that do not pay off are seen as mistakes and treated more as failures than opportunities to learn.

Some may argue that that is just the real world in operation, and of course, encouraging caution in your people may *not* result in the immediate demise of your organization. In certain circumstances it is highly desirable.

However, it *may* be a significant opportunity lost; not just in the market-place but to really engage the hearts and minds of your people in creating and implementing exciting new ideas, for example. The spin-offs can be considerable. If handled sympathetically, new insights, ideas and ways of doing things can release bursts of positive energy which spread round the organization, not only enhancing performance, but also creating new healthy social capital which is both self-reinforcing and fit for our times.

That is not to suggest that each employee should have the right to bet the firm as one notorious banker did a few years back. Rather, they should know where their boundaries are, what freedom exists within them and what to do when the boundaries start to impede progress. Chapter 4 deals with this concept in Fields of Freedom. In this respect, the role of the line manager is critical as they have the power to switch off the current on the risk and innovation circuit with remarkably little effort. A few negative words can do it. Body language and even silence can do it. When that happens, the fine words in company value statements are readily exposed for what they are by the deeds of managers on the ground. Actual organizational policy is always the one people experience, which may or may not coincide with the officially published version!

The challenge is to create a place where risk, creativity and innovation are seen as ways to increase one's standing in the community and not the reverse, where people feel supported and able to find the courage and resolve necessary to take the personal risks associated with breaking new ground in any arena of working life, where risks that do not pay off are valued every bit as highly as those that do, where wacky ideas are prized for the insights they bring – even if sometimes they don't.

The opportunity and pay-off is to release any untapped geyser of creative ideas and innovative action which is currently lying stifled within the human resource of the organization, to engage the hearts and minds of the people in creating and introducing new ways, new ideas, new deals and to really value their attempts to do so.

Loyalty and the confusion it creates

The old loyalty deal is dead and gone – if it ever existed. The new psychological contract between many employers and employed is founded in short-term contracts, mergers, delayering, expectations of mobility, short shelf-lives for hard-won skills, longer hours with little thought for personal lives, more change and stress, more buy-in specialists and less core employees, less time to get to know people beyond the superficial level and more uncertainty. And these may all be acceptable things, or at least appropriate things, but they have nothing to do with blind loyalty, which was the product of conditioning in a very different society. If instead, loyalty was ever the product of an unspoken contract where two parties gave it in fair exchange for certain behaviour or treatment, then that too is gone. Incidentally, if you want to see how it is done nowadays, many top managers give an excellent demonstration of how to play the modern game as they move on to fresh pastures every two or three years, sometimes faster.

The *Oxford English Dictionary* defines loyalty as being faithful in allegiance. It is an expression which conjures up employment for life, company towns, faithful servants and the like. It is supporting your local football team through thick and thin. It is hearts and minds stuff. Some attraction, some nostalgia then, but does loyalty still have a place in modern industry? We rather think it does not, at least in its old form. Nor in truth is it essential for the creation of healthy social capital. Just as well really, because all that any lingering nostalgia left in the collective consciousness of organizations *can* do, is cause confusion, and yet there remains this niggling expectation that people should be loyal to the firm!

By creating the kind of terms and conditions that they do, many organizations invite detachment not engagement on the part of employees at all levels. The psychological contract between organizations and the people they employ has changed so radically and perhaps irrevocably, that it is time for an explicit and honest new deal in this area. If the economic necessity is for short-term contracts and all the other conditions listed earlier, then organizations have to find other ways than traditional loyalty to engage their workforce.

The answer lies in creating systems of interaction which foster feelings of ownership and responsibility. In any organization, everyone is linked to some vital others whose co-operation or the lack of it can seriously make or mar their day, their ability to perform well and how they feel about themselves and their work. Individuals are linked to these vital others by arteries and for each person the pattern is different. It is the health of these arteries which offers the prospect of a workforce which feels fully engaged in the pursuit of the organization's goals.

The unique pattern of arteries for each individual or small functional group represents their true community of interest. If we are still trying to squeeze loyalty somewhere into our organization, it is here where its modern equivalent lies. To meet the demands of today, the replacement for traditional loyalty must be a two way street. Like trust, it must be earned and naturally it would also be really helpful if it was linked to performance outcomes.

In creating these conditions we must also be aware of, and be prepared to tackle, those feelings of community of interest which currently *do* seem to exist, but which often take a destructive form and produce counterproductive results. These occur where people choose to identify with perceived communities of interest which then operate in ways that are inconsistent with the delivery of maximum performance in the whole. We find this in functional units such as Finance, Human Resources, Engineering, R&D –

pretty well anywhere in fact. We even find it where office layout and proximity of desks at least offer people the time, space and opportunity for some daily contact. It is a testimony to the strength of humanity's need to belong that this occurs even when units rarely stay intact for more than a few months at a time, but it is a poor and inefficient way of going on. The ties that bind are loose because they are not founded on real common goals. They are weak because they have not really been earned and they are not well suited to withstand any serious assault by reality. Consequently, when some problem or threat emerges people are quick to revert to their own agendas. And who can blame them?

If as it seems, loyalty is a sub-plot in the need to belong, then organizations will benefit hugely from focusing this need on the delivery of their goals instead of the pursuit of partisan advantage. Rather than the vague pursuit of loyalty to an intangible entity then, we offer community of interest, founded on the experience of daily interactions, focused on common or compatible goals and leading to efficient interdependence and commonwealth.

The challenge is to offer an experience which harnesses people's energies in the pursuit of common goals – and in so doing creates a workforce committed to delivering overall success for the community of interest that the organization represents. It is time for organizations to play honestly by the rules and to admit openly that there really is no deal now on offer, which includes loyalty to the organization as a right.

The opportunity and pay-off is to attract the best people, who come because they have heard that yours is an organization where they will be valued and treated as responsible adults – and soon they will want to stay because they identify with the climate they now find themselves a part of, and they will come to look on the organization as theirs. Loyalty by another name? Could be. Certainly much more in tune with our times and our current needs.

Building community: why try?

So what are the arguments for organizations spending time, effort and money on making work a more satisfying place for humans to act and interact.

First, if you are up for a bit of reciprocal altruism, there would be a significant benefit to society which, by many measures, is now in some trouble. There will also be significant benefits closer to home. In almost all organizations, performance is the key driver. It may be sales or service, finance or quality, profit or profile, but ultimately organizations exist to deliver on their business targets. To do so consistently over time, organizations must maximize the use of their resources and minimize their costs. In saying this, it is not our intention to play down the importance of other considerations such as identifying a market niche, getting the pricing policy right, selecting the right products, cultivating strategic alliances and so on. These and many more can be vital to success. Rather, it is our argument that the difference in the quality of the execution of all these vital signs is down to people, and ultimately how much of themselves they are prepared to put into the organization they work for.

The challenge and the opportunity we offer is for leaders to create the kind of work experience which attracts and keeps the best people; and not just keeps them, but engages them as whole beings, who are committed to making their maximum contribution to the successful future of the organization they feel they belong in.

These people might not be easy to manage. They may care too much. They may demand more involvement and understanding. They may believe you when you ask them to take risks. They may argue with your solutions. You will find that commitment does not necessarily mean compliance. You will find that targets and methods are hotly debated and that your carefully thought out tactics are altered beyond recognition. You may spend as much time holding people back as you now spend pushing them forward. That can be personally frustrating but it is also a rewarding problem to have. It is far easier to temper people's enthusiasm with realism than it is to create it from nothing.

In this context, the Navigator is the visionary hero, the person who provides the inspiration by giving the direction, the long view, the wide perspective. The Flight Crew are the enablers who help the body of the organization to integrate, co-ordinate, co-operate and harmonize the different contributions in ways which best deliver overall success. The Core are responsible for engaging the majority of the organization's resources, human and otherwise, in the pursuit of high performance and success. This is a new role which must be actively and energetically encouraged, whilst at the same time crushing any attempts to return to the comfortable old preoccupations of control. The rest is all engine; an intelligent, robust, self-repairing, self-sustaining and self-improving engine which delivers the goods – the Activators. You will hear the roar and feel the surge when the engine engages.

This book is about the opportunity that leaders have now, to create organizations which reflect the latent power of thousands of years of evolution, but which at the same time meet modern expectations and deliver excellent performance.

Health check on social capital

In my organization:

Self-interest and sense of community are appropriately balanced. — I Agree/I Disagree

People show their willingness on a daily basis to commit and contribute to the greater good even when that means sacrificing partisan interests. — I Agree/I Disagree

People demonstrate their willingness on a daily basis to commit and to contribute all they are capable of to the greater good in exchange for a feeling that they belong – that they are a part of something. — I Agree/I Disagree

The whole workforce is tuned into the organization's goals and differentiated activities, and individual contributions are naturally integrated by effective daily interactions, allowing fast action, economic internal processes, quick responses and far-sightedness. — I Agree/I Disagree

The big picture is widely understood and everyone works towards it without regard to parochial advantage. — I Agree/I Disagree

There is a strong enough sense of belonging to the whole. — I Agree/I Disagree

Any competition that exists is productive. — I Agree/I Disagree

Co-operation between different functions is high. — I Agree/I Disagree

The leader inspires, generates passion and leads the charge toward the achievement of the organization's goals. — I Agree/I Disagree

Managers at all levels know they have the license to lead and use it appropriately. — I Agree/I Disagree

The role of manager as coach is highly valued. — I Agree/I Disagree

Managers spend far more time on looking up and out and managing their people for future performance than they do on daily routine tasks. — I Agree/I Disagree

Managers are actively encouraged and rewarded for concentrating on strategy and people management. — I Agree/I Disagree

Inspiring leadership behaviour is typical of our people at all levels and you can see it every day. — I Agree/I Disagree

Senior managers spend a lot of their time integrating and harmonizing and making sure the appropriate behaviours are used.	I Agree/I Disagree
People have time to get to know key others well enough to work together with maximum efficiency.	I Agree/I Disagree
We do not waste time, effort and money on avoidable monitoring and control.	I Agree/I Disagree
We share information, expertise and talent freely and trust is demonstrably high.	I Agree/I Disagree
We recognize and reward both individual and collective achievement.	I Agree/I Disagree
Risk, creativity and innovation are seen as ways to increase one's standing in the community and not the reverse.	I Agree/I Disagree
Risks that do not pay off are valued every bit as highly as those that do.	I Agree/I Disagree
Risks are calculated, planned and actively resourced.	I Agree/I Disagree
There are clear new valuable roles for managers to replace their old control functions.	I Agree/I Disagree
People understand their scope for initiative and how to work it legitimately.	I Agree/I Disagree
People feel able to contract directly and spontaneously with key others to obtain improvements in working efficiency.	I Agree/I Disagree
We attract and keep the best people.	I Agree/I Disagree
The social capital is extremely healthy.	I Agree/I Disagree
We have a highly effective working climate which is robust, self-sustaining and self-improving.	I Agree/I Disagree

There are twenty-eight questions. How many did you disagree with?

Chapter 2

Key Interactions

*Trust is like a lubricant that makes the running of any group or
organisation more efficient*
FRANCIS FUKUYAMA

*Reciprocity, moral obligation, duty toward community and
trust are founded in habit*
FRANCIS FUKUYAMA

Here's tae us and wha's like us. Damn few and they're a' deid!
A SCOTTISH TOAST

It seems clear that, within most of humanity, there exists a deep-seated need
to belong, but it does not exist in isolation. There is another powerful driver;
an opposing force, which creates a dynamic tension in our activities. It is the
pursuit of self-interest. Indeed, one of the arguments upon which this book
is founded, is that the latter is rather more apparent and at home in the daily
affairs of modern humanity, than the former.

It is not our contention that one is good and the other is bad, but
rather that both exist, and that any temporary ascendancy that one might
enjoy over the other in their perpetual power struggle will have a significant
effect on the state of health of the social capital in any given society or
organization.

Perhaps it is the presence of these two adversaries that helps make
humankind such a dangerously successful creature. Both are certainly
capable of making either positive or negative contributions. For its part,
self-interest can stimulate individual ambition and the pursuit of personal

goals and can lead to positive outcomes such as self-actualization and leaps of creative imagination as well as to less productive, more divisive pursuits. The need to belong can lead to unproductive herd behaviour, where mediocrity reigns, just as much as it can produce exciting synergy and an appropriate willingness to subordinate self-interest to the achievement of the greater good.

This chapter addresses the need to identify and then create the right mix of these two powerful and conflicting drives within an organization, and so produce a climate where excellent performance is the dominant preoccupation of everyone.

Today, within the societies of many developed countries, particularly those based on the western model, there appears to be an imbalance in favour of self-interest. For example, there is a view that in Britain, social capital is in serious decline – that the consensus of what constitutes moral standards and civilized behaviour appears to be breaking up. One statistic offered in support of this argument is Britain's crime rate, which, excluding homicide, has risen significantly in recent years. In the USA, some commentators suggest that the rising tide of individualism and its concomitant, the lowering of sociability in American society at large, is associated with a general sense amongst the population, of a lack of shared values and community with those around them – in other words, a depletion of healthy social capital. As a result, Americans are said to be paying significantly more than other industrialized countries for civil protection.

That does not sound like good economics. It also raises the question of what may be happening in the organizations that are part of those societies and which inevitably must both affect and be affected by the wider social trends taking place there. If a sense of belonging is not active in an organization, then that organization is likely to have to use increased amounts of monitoring and control in order to succeed. Managers will therefore spend more time with their eyes focused down on operational issues and less time looking up, around and ahead. Workers feel they are not responsible or answerable, and act accordingly, withdrawing their initiative and creativity.

Exactly what inspires individuals to give more of themselves in exchange for the benefits of membership of any given community depends very much on the individual, and probably the list of motivators is almost endless. There may well be people who choose to operate almost exclusively in either the self-interest or the community camp, but these people are relatively rare. What concerns us here are the preferences of the majority, where the desire to pursue individual gratification is tempered with the need to belong. It is here that action on the part of organizations can pay significant dividends.

If we were entirely logical and calculating beings we might conclude that sometimes it is worthwhile to make sacrifices for the greater good and sometimes it is not. This is the 'utility' argument, and, if verbalized, it might go something like this. 'When a community attains enough standing, it becomes worth my being a member. In order to be a member I will have to make some apparently altruistic moves. It will be worth the effort for the benefits membership will bring a little further down the line.' Of course, this verbalization does not usually take place, even in our thoughts. If it did, it would be frowned upon. It would not be considered respectable, and yet it may be more appropriate to the conditions in which many people now find themselves in medium to large organizations than the reciprocal altruism we discussed in Chapter 1. However distasteful, it may be that the honest and productive way of doing collective business today is through just such a conscious process. What *is* clear is that the dynamic tension between self and community interests is in need of a thorough overhaul.

While, as we have observed, some degree of self-interest can be productive, there is also an increasing need for collective effectiveness as people's lives become ever more complex, 'sophisticated' and, well, just fast! Society is more specialized, our gadgets are more inscrutable and our demand for an efficient supporting cast in the shape of the service sector seems insatiable. We need our cappuccinos, but we don't really have the time, the technology or the inclination to make a good one ourselves. We are highly interdependent and it appears we are becoming more so by the hour. Yet some powerful new forces seem to be stoking the fires of fragmentation. Does e-mail, for instance, enhance or detract from our feelings of connection to our colleagues? The answer is probably a bit of both, but, despite its benefits, is e-mail a real replacement for face-to-face contact? Likewise homeworking, contracting out of non-core services, and short or fixed term contracts – all seem to be working to the current disadvantage of our sense of connection and belonging. It doesn't feel right. It is not how we produce our best work; at least, not over a sustained period. These things are not bad in themselves, but they have rocked the boat. The right mix needs to be restored.

Organizations face many demands on their limited time and energies. It is important that they get maximum return from any investment they make in trying to fix the mix. Activities aimed at improving performance through increased collective effectiveness should pay their way from day one. Later in this chapter we offer one way which has proved successful. We call it Key Interactions.

Before we go there, however, some readers may want to explore in a little more detail these two opposing forces, these protagonists, and consider the power struggle they have been engaged in probably since humanity began.

The need to belong to a community of interest

Part of the desire for belonging is obviously founded in the success that co-operative action delivers. From hunting mammoths to sophisticated political faction fights, it has always helped to have more people with you fighting your corner than the opposition. Relative numbers frequently count and most days can swamp those wimps like right and morality – which is just fine because then you don't have to worry too much about all that intellectual argument stuff. So much the better if you happen to have right on your side, but big numbers do the business either way – the good old 'might is right' philosophy.

Of course, human resources are not the only significant numbers that affect the outcomes of our collective interactions. Traditionally, in addition to family, tribe and allies, numbers of power have included assorted livestock, for example. And since that form of commercial tender has rather passed into history, not least because of the difficulty of giving change, we naturally looked around for other currencies. Acreage was fashionable for a while and indeed it still has a small but faithful following in many regions. Money will always be a firm favourite, of course. Then we have power and influence themselves. Although difficult to quantify, this dynamic pair usually comes down to numbers of some kind in the end, if you care to probe just a wee bit below the surface. Hence, one powerful backer with some suitable numbers in their locker can sometimes outweigh a sizeable community in terms of clout. So, regardless of what happens to be in vogue, numbers have always figured directly and effectively in the process of human interactions, and the number of people following a common interest is always a factor.

Yet numbers and the success they bring are not the only reason why the need to belong is a powerful player in human nature. History, and indeed daily life, is liberally endowed with examples of smaller numbers overcoming larger. What is that about then? Words like spirit and camaraderie spring to mind. Sometimes it just feels good to be a part of a collection of people who want the same things or have the same interests or talk and think like us, look like us or whatever. It may just feel good not to be the only one with the creative body piercing! Clubs of all sorts reflect this although most require less surgical spirit, and because of these similarities, when something needs to be done, we will be likely to co-operate with our 'club-mates'. It is a bit like being part of a family but with less binding ties and without eccentric old Uncle Jim – although not necessarily.

There is also the vital ingredient of collective perception and emotion. People who are interacting well and who feel they are a community can often convince themselves that something is possible which, if they had time to sit down and think about on their own for a few minutes, would result in them sloping quietly off to undertake some less hazardous venture. Instead, they go charging away together to attempt the impossible, or even just the really unlikely and jings, crivvens (Scottish vernacular expression indicating extreme astonishment), sometimes they do it! It seems that collective chemistry can override rational thought and allow people to attempt new and risky things. As such it is a powerful force which can achieve some really dramatic and positive results.

Results against the odds are always hugely satisfying and that gives rise to yet another argument for belonging. Positive, collective performance produces a community identity and a reputation. The community attains a standing in the eyes of others which is separate from its individual members, but which reflects favourably on each individual as well. Members bask in the collective achievement and frequently change the way they behave as individuals to conform more to the community image. This is part of the power of reputation, which is discussed in more detail in Chapter 1, but there is more. Not only does a positive image cause people to start to behave differently, it also acts as a strong encouragement to members to repeat those behaviours which are the focus of such internal or external approval. Their self-image begins to change. The experience can even reach to the centre of one's being, although, to be effective in the organizational context, it need not do so.

So, co-operation and a sense of 'us' has a beneficial effect on outcomes because it feels good, offers some form of numerical advantage, encourages boldness when faced with bad odds, enhances the standing of individual members, activates society's reputation mechanism and makes us feel better about ourselves to the extent that sometimes we may even feel compelled to live up to the image.

All is not rosy in the collective garden of course. Naturally there are some negatives to offset the positives. Things do not always go well, and when the chemistry goes bad, the consequences can be very destructive. The quality of interactions deteriorates, information ceases to flow, barriers are built and people leave either physically or emotionally, resulting in poor performance and sometimes the effective disintegration of the community. Even when this extreme form does not manifest itself, things can still go wrong in the collective arena. Working closely allows individuals and groups to draw comparisons between rewards received and contributions made, and gives scope for feelings of unfair treatment. Furthermore, any process involving numbers of people has the capacity to become frustrating, slow and boring. Handled badly, the experience can dampen the fires of enthusiasm, stifle creativity and inhibit innovative action. Even that otherwise praiseworthy willingness to tackle impossible odds can be a dangerous detachment from reality, a lemming-like form of group hysteria.

Whatever the pros and cons, collective effectiveness is obviously an important factor in success or failure. In today's complex and interdependent environment, organizations are clearly right to spend time working to make sure people interact effectively within and between groups as well as individually. When things go wrong in the collective arena, organizations frequently turn to team building. Right instinct, wrong solution, but before we consider the alternative, we need to address the opposing force of self-interest.

The pursuit of self-interest

Economists might argue that every person is actuated primarily by self-interest. That seems too sweeping but observation *does* suggest that most people pursue their own selfish interests rather more often than not, at least more often than they behave altruistically and contribute to the common wealth of the community. Some of the great and good who study such things for a living believe that a model of human behaviour, based on rationality and self-interest, would apply about 80% of the time. They may well be right in crude quantitative terms, but leaders of organizations, who must live with the consequences of their actions, should be wary. Community-driven behaviours, whilst less frequent, may reach further down into our humanity than their incidence suggests. Nonetheless it is undeniable that self-interest is a major motivator for humanity and that it looms large in everything we do.

One manifestation lies in our propensity to compete for limited anything. There may be differences between cultures and there are arguably differences between genders, but we are on reasonably safe ground when we conclude that human beings are competitive animals. In Darwinian terms, that is how some survived to pass on their genes and some did not. There is of course a counter argument to the survival of the fittest, for those of you who are familiar with the arguments surrounding the Burgess Shales, but luck and being in the right place at the right time are perhaps something for another book. At any rate, when we compete with others, it is safe to say that mostly we do so for ourselves as individuals or some collective we think of as 'us'.

As our world has become more complex and sophisticated, so the things we compete for have changed to reflect our progress. Instead of mammoth meat or territory (although, come to think of it, territory is still quite popular and may get a new lease of life with the advent of global warming), people quickly moved to compete for wealth, status, quality of life, power, public acclaim, private affection and so on. Naturally, in the organizations which make these sophisticated worlds possible, we compete as well, and largely for the same things.

One of the things we compete for is reward – pay for instance. In organizations, there has been a trend to link pay and performance as directly as possible. This is understandable, but it certainly has the effect of reinforcing the case for self-interest by focusing the endeavours of individuals on their own performance. If the case were to be thought through consciously and rationally, it would go something like this. 'If it is important to show how well I am performing and why I should be the one who is successful in competing for the scarce resource of that pay rise or that promoted post, then I would be wise to act accordingly. I may, for instance, have some information which is useful, but I will keep it to myself so that I will be able to use it to my advantage. I don't wish my colleagues any harm, you understand, but if someone is going to benefit, then it might as well be me. I am, after all, the most deserving case I know.' Mostly, of course, it isn't that explicit or conscious. Such conversations may go on in some unconscious part of our brain, which recognizes the signs and steers its host in the direction its evolutionary survival mechanisms have found to work over the millennia, but to express such sentiments would be no more acceptable in polite society than our thoughts on utility, and would indeed be counterproductive in any case. No matter. For organizations, it is the management of the behaviour itself that holds the key.

The challenge and the opportunity for organizations is to consider whether they couldn't benefit significantly by mixing their signals a bit more to include some incentives which resonate better with our need to feel included, to be a recognized part of something. Some will say they do so already by including in their appraisal systems, such behavioural targets relating to team working and interpersonal skills. There will also be some fine words in vision and/or values statements, but, if you think those are more than just words, you should listen at more keyholes. So often it is the case that the Flight Crew and the Core pay only lip service to these 'soft' targets, and grudging lip service at that. What people know to be the real truth is what they experience in others' behaviour. What is needed, in order to really get the message over, is deeds. Turning the good intentions into practical observable reality is the essence of the Key Interactions process we describe on pp. 44–56.

From the point of view of organizational performance, the question of whether the pursuit of self-interest is right or wrong, is largely irrelevant. The fact is that it is a major player in the behaviour of working people and must be managed in an effective way. It is a part of us and is the source of as many positive outcomes as negative. The desire to be all we can be, to use our talents, to engage in experiences which maximize our sense of achievement, self-worth and *joie de vivre*, are all capable of making very positive contributions to the interactions between ourselves and others, and incidentally to the wealth and welfare of the whole.

Tackling the mix to deliver healthy social capital

There are powerful drives, founded in our evolutionary history, both for belonging within a community and for the pursuit of self-interest. There are also strong intellectual and empirical arguments for the effectiveness of collective co-operation to set against the obvious benefits deriving from the pursuit of personal success and recognition. These drives tend to live together in an uneasy truce, which from time to time erupts into hostilities. If the mix is wrong the organization will be inefficient.

Therefore, when self-interest assumes too great a weight in our affairs, as it has done in recent years, organizations are wise to take action. It is not good enough to adopt policies which say implicitly to their people, 'We will pay and reward you as individuals but you should work like a community.' Rather they must find ways to blend the two opposing drives of belonging and self-interest in ways which benefit organization, individual, and, incidentally, society at large.

The economic argument is straightforward. The need for inclusion and a sense of belonging is there just waiting to be tapped. In return, people will contribute more of themselves to something they feel a genuine part of. And great news! There is a gap in the market caused by society's inability to meet that need. It is only waiting for someone to take advantage and fill it with the right mix to produce healthy and productive social capital and enhanced organizational performance.

Team building – not the best solution to the problem

One of the ways that organizations frequently try to tackle these conflicting drives and pressures is by engaging in team building. On the face of it, the case for organizations making this kind of investment would seem sound. *Something* has to be done to redress the balance! They must be pushing against an already half open door, and yet, curiously, team building as an activity *per se*, is not the right tool for this particular job. The return on such investment is inefficient at best. At worst, it is a waste of time and money which diverts attention and energy away from the key preoccupations of business – performance and results.

The time for engaging in team building activities is when people who are working together start to complain that they 'could do much better if only!!!' If you can anticipate their cries by a day or two, then well done you. Only then will the activity produce a consistently good return on investment, because the outcomes will be owned by the participants and directly linked to immediate and sustainable pay-offs in improved performance, pleasanter less hostile working relationships, stronger positive feelings about the community of interest and higher self-esteem.

More specifically, the problem we see with team building as an organizational activity is that it often lacks a sense of immediate relevance to, and impact on, day-to-day business in the hearts and minds of those participating. That is not the intention of those sponsoring the team building initiative of course, who might well argue that their primary objective is better performance. Yet despite the unquestioned quality of many team building experiences, participants often carry with them a feeling that they have other more important things to do, and would probably rather be somewhere else if given complete freedom of choice. Some of them are indeed somewhere else despite apparent corporeal evidence to the contrary. Just watch them dive for their cellphones at every break! That absence of practical and direct application, whether perceived or real, can create a feeling amongst participants that team building is an end-goal itself. As a result, the outcome of the activity is a house built on sand, which lacks the structural integrity and robustness to be able to cope successfully and triumph over the many forms of adversity it must inevitably encounter in modern organizational life.

When trouble arrives in the shape of failure or poor performance, when the different pictures people carry about collective objectives prove to be just too different, when perceptions grow that there is a mismatch between some individual's contribution and the reward they are getting – then teams, which have been formed into teams because teams seem like a good thing to form into, are in trouble. They have no process to fall back on because the process which formed the team in the first place was not driven by real need and was therefore far too vague.

Teams built out of good intentions simply do not have the equipment to get themselves out of trouble. On the other hand, if people can build up effective ways of interacting with each other, so that they can deliver specific outcomes and in so doing feel good about themselves and the people around them, then they will have all the tools they need. They will have the accepted norms of behaviour which were applied to the situation in which they first found themselves before they got things going last time. They will have the key interpersonal skills they had then too, although now these will have been honed by constant practice in dealing with those small bumps in the road we all encounter each day. Whenever they find themselves with a real crisis to deal with or a difficult new initiative to drive forward, they will be raring to tackle it and equipped to win; and when they do, they will know how good it feels to win in good company.

If organizations aspire to low maintenance (i.e. with the minimum of monitoring and controls), high performance interactions, then they have to build collective effectiveness out of the business and human needs which are the active ingredients at their disposal. Against the background of the current trends in society and the employment market, it is unrealistic, inefficient and counterproductive to attempt to build traditional team spirit. Instead, the appropriate contemporary route to a sense of community interest is through honest, upfront, well negotiated, market deals; deals which embody respect and trust.

A way forward

In essence, the healthy working environment of the near future must offer conditions where excellent performance is robust, self-sustaining and self-improving. This is possible in a climate rich in healthy social capital, where the mix of self-interest and sense of community is right, but how to bring this about?

What is required is a process which allows anyone at any time to initiate action to tackle any interaction that is materially affecting their ability to deliver excellent performance; a process which recognizes and works with the interdependencies which exist, without implying that everyone should feel guilty if they don't feel like one big team; a process which effects the necessary improvements, whilst at the same time maintaining or enhancing the working relationship with other parties just enough to be sure that the deal will last. Because that is what the process is – a market deal; one based on a high level of interpersonal skills, but a market deal nonetheless (see Chapter 6 for details of the process). The aim is to generate collective effectiveness by equipping everyone to create the conditions which work best for them whilst at the same time keeping the success of the whole organization in view.

In this way the benefits of collective action can be attained whilst at the same time making it acceptable to pursue personal success and recognition. Above all else, such a process must enable people to deliver consistently excellent performance with the minimum of time and effort spent on policing and control. Then, if genuine teams *do* materialize in time, at least they will be the result of legitimate efforts to deliver the organization's goals, and not through the pursuit of the, at best, troubled vision of the good things of being part of a team.

The following checklists are provided to help make connections between the points raised in this chapter and the reality in your own organization. Try them now or skip them till you need them later as you wish. A description of the Key Interactions process itself comes right after.

Checklist

These questions relate to the key messages from the first part of this chapter.

In my organization:

The mix of self-interest and sense of community is about right.   I Agree/I Disagree

Excellent performance is the preoccupation of everyone.   I Agree/I Disagree

Managers do not spend too much time on monitoring and controlling day-to-day operations.	I Agree/I Disagree
People at all levels feel they have a responsibility for the overall success of the organization and they act accordingly.	I Agree/I Disagree
Our reward and recognition systems encourage collective co-operation just as much as they do individual achievement.	I Agree/I Disagree
Our collective actions are never ponderous, slow or boring.	I Agree/I Disagree
Interactions between individuals and between groups are of a consistently high quality, demonstrated by the contribution the outcomes make to overall performance.	I Agree/I Disagree
Any team building activities we have undertaken in the past 3 years have contributed directly to improved performance and have represented an excellent return on the overall investment made.	I Agree/I Disagree
People deliver consistently excellent performance with minimal policing and control.	I Agree/I Disagree

If you either answered Disagree or perhaps wished there was a 'maybe' category, then Key Interactions may make a significant difference to the introduction of healthier social capital in your organization, as well as improving its overall performance.

The Key Interactions process

The Key Interactions process is an engine for effecting a major step change in performance and then holding onto it. These questions may help you determine what specific ways of working which currently prevail within your organization would benefit from the application of the Key Interactions process.

Checklist

In my organization:

Everyone takes responsibility for ensuring s/he is clear what their own objectives mean, how they fit with the wider picture of corporate/department/ unit objectives and how they impact on key others.	I Agree/I Disagree

People actively manage the processes and relationships which are essential to their ability to deliver results.	I Agree/I Disagree
People respond positively when approached by someone seeking their co-operation to improve performance.	I Agree/I Disagree
People wishing to improve performance spontaneously identify and seek to involve all other interested parties regardless of status.	I Agree/I Disagree
People at all levels readily cross functional boundaries and break old taboos in order to solve problems and improve productivity.	I Agree/I Disagree
People understand the licence they have to take initiatives and they exercise that licence to the full each day.	I Agree/I Disagree
People know the key others they need to interact with to enable them to maximize their contribution to the organization's success.	I Agree/I Disagree
Key relationships are typified by co-operative, effective and efficient interactions.	I Agree/I Disagree
The desire to improve collective performance is demonstrably at the forefront of everyone's motivation.	I Agree/I Disagree
Factional interests and gains are invariably subordinated to the wider company good in our day-to-day working.	I Agree/I Disagree
Any competition that exists between functions serves only to enhance collective effectiveness.	I Agree/I Disagree
Everyone, not just the manager, thinks strategically as well as operationally.	I Agree/I Disagree

If you either answered Disagree or perhaps wished there was a 'maybe' category, then Key Interactions may make a significant difference to the introduction of healthier social capital in your organization, as well as improving its overall performance.

The process in overview

Frances Fukuyama, in his book *Trust – The Social Virtues and Creation of Prosperity*, suggests that 'choices influenced by culture arise out of habit', rather than rational calculations of self-interest. The Key Interactions process offers a way of generating that *habit* – the habit of tackling any situation where the quality of the interaction required, whether it be product, service, information, accessibility or whatever, is below standard; the habit of tackling these issues in ways which result not only in performance improvements which benefit the wider organization, but also at least maintain and at best enhance the future working relationship between the negotiating parties; the habit of trusting people with an honest revelation of problems and feelings and respecting those revelations by others.

The primary aim is unashamedly to deliver the benefits of collective effectiveness to the organization. But that aim is inextricably linked with the feelings and needs of the people who make that organization what it is. At first glance, Key Interactions may seem a hard-nosed, cold and calculating process, focused entirely on satisfying selfish task needs, but the appearance is deceptive. The process requires those involved to treat each other with courtesy, respect and honesty and in so doing gives rise to reciprocity, moral obligation and new levels of trust and empathy. Albeit just enough to get a result, but what more is really necessary?

The Key Interactions process concentrates on the delivery of valued and valuable improvements in ways of working (this covers systems, personal relationships, communications, information streams, technical aspects and more) by requiring the players to address those interactions which are key to their ability to achieve excellent performance. To make this work, it uses the mechanistic (market deals) approach we discuss in Chapters 1 and 6, supported by the creation of a set of interpersonal behavioural norms.

The introductory phase, which lasts approximately four weeks, comprises the following stages:

1   Individuals and homogeneous functional subgroups within units are asked to identify the four or five working relationships which are key to their ability to successfully deliver excellent performance.

2   They then address the quality of the interactions which epitomize these relationships and describe how they are now and how they should be in future.

3   They then plan and begin to take action to eliminate the easiest looking discrepancies by closing the gap between the actual and should-be states. The essence is to start on small-scale issues involving one-to-one contracting. This builds good feelings of success, creates momentum and offers low-threat opportunities to build up expertise in the process. The first results are immediate.

The secondary phase, which lasts until the behaviours become the norm, involves the following activities:

1   Individuals and homogeneous subgroups continue to tackle the key interactions which concern them. These activities are heavily supported by managerial coaching, facilitation and both formal and informal recognition.

2   Larger more complex issues begin to be tackled. The bigger and more wide-ranging the subject, the more interested parties are likely to become involved, and the more the negotiators will need the skills of project management and formal negotiating. Trust also becomes a more prominent feature as negotiators are given licence to speak for others in their unit. (See Field of Freedom and negotiating in Chapters 4 and 6, respectively.)

3   The new ways of working are spread through contact (e.g. managerial coaching and facilitation). The key role of Core managers in this is described in Chapters 4 and 6. Behavioural skills training should only be injected where the foregoing support mechanisms need additional support to make them work.

4   The new ways become the norm.

The following pages provide a more detailed, step-by-step description of how the process can be managed. If you have a particular preference for detail, then read on. Otherwise, the rest of the chapter is intended mainly for those who will be actively engaged in running the process itself.

The principal steps

Step 1: Ensuring the necessary behaviours, attitudes and skills are in place

In order to have maximum impact on performance and ways of working, the Key Interactions process demands that certain interpersonal tools (behaviours, attitudes and skills) are present in the target population so that they can be used in day-to-day interactions. If they are present, even if they are not used all that regularly, then you can move straight into the Key Interactions process proper. If they are not present or there are gaps, then you will need to create the skill base.

First then, it is necessary to carry out an assessment of the state of readiness of the population in relation to these tools. This process can be as simple or as complex as you like. We have provided a checklist for you to use in your audit, but you may wish to create one of your own which reflects exactly, the conditions currently prevailing in your organization.

The key tools, in no particular order, are:

• contracting with others and negotiating market deals (see Chapter 6);
• influencing and confronting assertively;

- dealing with 'difficult' people, handling conflict and emotionally charged situations positively, including resistance;
- listening and questioning, sensitivity to non-verbal signals, empathic behaviour;
- problem solving (task *and* people);
- working with staff, peers and senior management in a spontaneous project environment;
- planning and managing finite resources.

The aim is to create a critical mass of people and behaviours which produces a new way of working within the unit and beyond. To illustrate how these contribute to the Key Interactions process, here are a couple of examples:

1   Confronting assertively: We have found that people often use the term assertive to describe behaviours which in reality can only be viewed as aggressive. It is essential that people undertaking the Key Interactions process understand the difference, and have the skills to be assertive. If such confusion exists, it must be dealt with as part of a workshop activity. The skill of confronting is discussed in more detail in Chapter 6.

2   The skills of project management: These are vital to an organization which requires people to take ownership for managing their own work. To deliver the best results for the organization, they must:

- be prepared to challenge effectively (themselves and others) so that the project brief is fully understood and well thought through;
- be willing and able to see beyond their own patch and their short-term needs;
- be able to identify relevant others and pull together small interested groups if appropriate;
- have the tools necessary to work well with others from different functions and different levels;
- work in ways which both get results and enhance relationships for the future;
- be focused on producing the best overall outcome for the greater good and be fully prepared to sacrifice factional gains;
- know when to disband the group.

The following checklist may help you assess the extent to which the people in your organization already exhibit the essential behaviours necessary to implement the Key Interactions process successfully.

Checklist

Skills, behaviours and attitudes

In my organization:

When faced with a difficulty with another person's work, people   I Agree/I Disagree
will usually speak to the person concerned rather than griping
to the boss or anyone else who will listen, or just putting up
with the poor standard of interaction.

When they need someone to change a way of working or   I Agree/I Disagree
behaving so that they can do their jobs more effectively
and get better results, people tackle the issue in ways
which not only get the desired result but also enhance
the working relationship and the effectiveness of any
future interactions.

In discussions and conversations, people typically show good   I Agree/I Disagree
listening behaviour and ask the kind of questions which
help ensure they really understand the other person better,
both factually and emotionally.

When considering a course of action that might impact on   I Agree/I Disagree
others, people automatically take steps to engage the other's
interest and active involvement.

People show a keen awareness of the talents and experience   I Agree/I Disagree
available in any group they happen to be working with, and
use these skilfully for the greatest good, regardless of
differences in formal status.

When people encounter resistance they do not try to squash it   I Agree/I Disagree
or ignore it, but, instead, tackle it honestly and directly and with
such skills that the result is a better solution with the prospect
of better and more productive future working relationships.

When working on a collective task or problem, all parties take   I Agree/I Disagree
care to try to see each other's point of view and have the
motivation, the behavioural skills and the process tools to
find the best solution for the organization and not just the
best for their patch.

People have a range of effective problem-solving tools in their   I Agree/I Disagree
behavioural toolbox.

People have the behavioural skills to handle emotional or   I Agree/I Disagree
difficult people situations in ways which produce enhanced
future working relationships as well as good practical outcomes.

People understand the finite nature of resources and tackle collective issues with those in mind.	I Agree/I Disagree
People know how to plan both operationally and strategically.	I Agree/I Disagree
People are constantly alert for new ways of working, systems and techniques and see these as opportunities for improvement rather than an inconvenience.	I Agree/I Disagree
Everyone that needs them has the interpersonal skills to tackle Key Interactions effectively.	I Agree/I Disagree

If you either answered Disagree or perhaps wished there was a 'maybe' category, then Key Interactions may make a significant difference to the introduction of healthier social capital in your organization, as well as improving its overall performance, but you will have to consider training before taking it further.

Step 2: Designing and delivering whatever training is required

In the interests of speed and cost-effectiveness, training at this time should be restricted to those units who will be directly engaged in the Key Interactions process. The net can be widened later as necessary, but the aim is to avoid unnecessary expenditure on training, and instead to spread the new ways of working as much as possible by practical example.

Where training *is* required, we have found that short modular workshops produce the best results quickly. These are typically two consecutive days followed by some time for practice, 6 weeks or so, before the next subject is addressed in another 2 day workshop. This puts the real learning process into the workplace where it belongs, and encourages line managers to support and share in the journey. Optimum workshop size for chemistry is between twelve and sixteen participants with two experienced tutors. There are many variations possible in the timing, however, which can be influenced by the sophistication of the subject matter or the learning preferences of the participants.

Step 3: Developing the Key Interactions

If the target population already possesses the skills necessary for Key Interactions to work, then selecting the date to start is a matter solely of organizational convenience. Where some training in skill development is taking place however, there is an additional dynamic. Go too soon and the population do not have enough of the skills to make the process work; too late and the new tools may have dissipated for lack of a coherent vehicle. The aim, naturally, is to strike at the right time and so create a critical mass of new behaviours, solidly anchored in business reality, and giving immediate as well as long-term, valued pay-offs to the people and the organization.

The Key Interactions process starts when a work unit is asked to meet together for half a day. The whole of the unit need not attend but those who *must* be there are the Core manager, the unit manager and key members of the unit. The main functions of the unit must be represented. As the most economical number of participants for one facilitator to handle is twelve, it is perfectly fine, if small units are involved, to have more than one unit represented, provided all the other attendance criteria are met.

This first meeting will be followed by a second, a week later. The same people must be able to attend. The gap of a week is to allow time for reflection and for clarification of any elements from the first day's agenda. For example, Core manager goals sometimes need to be translated into practical examples in order to be truly helpful to those they impact upon.

The agenda shown below covers the action for both half-days, as progress is not uniform, with some groups moving rather faster through the early parts of the agenda than others for a number of reasons. The probable break point between what can be achieved in week 1 and week 2 is shown in italics. Over the two sessions, each functional unit should:

- come to a full understanding of what these sessions are trying to achieve;
- resolve their issues and questions, and air any 'baggage';
- refine and clarify their understanding of what individual, group and department objectives will mean in this new context of healthy social capital;
- debate what active management of Key Interactions really means, and create a commitment list of descriptions of active management behaviours to act as a constant checklist later in the process (a composite list is located at the end of this chapter);
- identify the few individuals or groups whose actions and performance are genuinely critical to their success;
- using a more or less standard change model, create descriptions of the nature and quality of the current state of the interactions including the health of the personal working relationships;
- continuing with the same model, create descriptions of how these same interactions and relationships should be.

This is often the break point between week 1 and 2

- identify what they will need to do to close the gap between the current and should-be states;
- produce realistic plans for negotiating and contracting initiatives, which will take place over the next two weeks;

- identify whose support they may need to make this happen;
- contract with the manager and key others for the exact nature of the support required (this can range from close support, through coaching, to 'get off my back');
- select negotiators where group interests are involved and contract for appropriate licence to negotiate;
- agree dates and times for the group to meet once again, and commit to personal targets to be achieved by then.

By the end of week 2 of the process, participants will have:

- a clear understanding of what organisation and unit objectives mean to their function and to them individually;
- a graphic representation which they have constructed themselves with the current and should-be states described in some detail for each of their key interactions;
- a commitment statement which they have developed with their manager about what behaviours both will need to exhibit to close each gap between the current and should-be states;
- a contract specifying the support the manager will give and an agreement about unsolicited interference;
- an agreed plan of action with firm steps and deadlines for contracting with key others to close the gaps between the current and should-be states;
- a statement of trust in any representatives embarking on larger scale negotiations;
- a date to meet in week 5 to celebrate progress, troubleshoot barriers and drive onwards.

Everyone should be actively engaged in progressing at least one contracting objective. Many may also be working in pairs or small groups to progress larger projects for themselves or on behalf of the whole group. As with any new behaviour, it is safer to start close to home. That is to say that people should be given the opportunity to practise within their own unit or immediate sphere of activity before they tackle the wider environment. You would not perhaps try out your new skills first on a key customer for instance. Where appropriate, some of these initial sessions can be facilitated by a trained facilitator from outside the unit (See Chapter 6).

Step 4: Putting Key Interactions into action – weeks 3 and 4

In weeks 3 and 4 there may be some early overtures for larger negotiating meetings, but for the most part activity will centre round facilitated one-to-one contracting sessions. These may be as short as 15 or 20 minutes or as long as a couple of hours. Each party shares their perceptions of the current and should-be state for a specific interaction and then both parties look for ways to close the gap. All the behaviours, attitudes and skills referred to on pp. 44–5 are potentially employed. Where early deals are possible they are done on the spot. People are often surprised how many of these small, immediate improvements are possible and the goodwill and momentum they generate. The outcomes from these sessions are mostly deals on specific ways of working between individuals and small scale but important changes in procedures and systems. Where the task is bigger or involves several other functions, these meetings often form the basis of a future project.

Not all successes come this easily however, and some require more work and more time. For instance, the negotiators may find that they need to widen the scope of their negotiations to include others. They may have too much 'bad history' between them to be able to sort things out themselves and may need help in resolving their conflicts. These are the kind of circumstances where the coaching, facilitative, perspective-giving roles of the Flight Crew and Core manager are so important.

Step 5: Secondary phase – driving and nurturing – as long as it takes

After week 4, people will sometimes feel they have made great progress. Others will become frustrated because either things are not moving as fast as they would like, or they find that all the old ways keep trying to creep back in. In the former condition, they often feel they can relax and try less hard. In the latter, they often feel the task is just too big for them and want to give up. Both conditions benefit from tough support delivered early. Examples are:

- Shortfalls in behavioural skills or knowledge must be identified early and rapidly addressed by coaching or training as appropriate.
- As the process gathers momentum, the Flight Crew should take an active interest and publicly recognize success and even effort.
- Peer support can be encouraged by the creation of learning sets.
- A high visibility, non-bureaucratic way of tracking progress on closing the gaps should be introduced and run by the participants themselves, who flag up successes to the Flight Crew for swift celebration and act as ambassadors, role models and progress chasers – almost as if the organization belonged to them in fact!

Step 6: The new norms

It becomes the norm for interested people to form spontaneously around a problem or idea or opportunity for effecting a performance or system improvement. They work on it, drawing in what help and expertise they need and when it is over, they disband.

The process in detail for facilitators

For the two half-day sessions the optimum workshop size for a trained facilitator is twelve participants. These must include the Core manager of the unit, the functional unit manager, plus other key staff so that all the major functions are properly represented. Where units with small numbers exist, they may be put together with another small unit to make the numbers up to twelve. An open U shape of seats, with or without small tables, works well. The process benefits from a plentiful supply of flip charts and plenty of wall space.

The process for week 1

Introduce the session objectives and walk through the process for the two half-days in a summarized form. Review these, checking for understanding, discussing how this part of the process fits with the whole and its relevance to the participants' real working environment and developing social capital. Agree how the participants should work together during the session, to ensure the objectives are met.

Split the group into threes or fours (if not already seated at small tables) to consider their unit and individual objectives, and to generate practical examples of how these should work in practice. Returning to whole group, discuss the objectives, using the practical examples to test their true meaning, particularly against the unit manager's interpretation. Agree the true interpretation of the objectives, writing down any which would benefit from such a record. If any issues or uncertainties remain, ask for some participants to take responsibility for clearing these up and reporting back to the week 2 session.

Now in whole group, either brainstorm a list of active management behaviours or critique the list at the end of this chapter. Use the list to test what the fine words mean in practice. One way to do this is to break into small groups, each taking a few behaviours and ask them to create small cameos of work situations to illustrate what each would mean in practice. Report out and debate as necessary to ensure everyone understands the behavioural expectations behind the process.

Ask participants to identify those few individuals, functions or units, whose actions and performance are genuinely critical to their success (four or five is

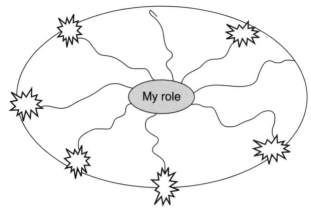

Figure 2.1. The bloodshot eye.

the maximum if the definition of critical is strictly applied as it must be). This is best done in subgroups of three or four. Functionally homogeneous membership is ideal. However, where individuals exist within a functional unit, who have quite distinct and different roles from the others, forming small syndicate groups composed of these singleton operators to work together and create the necessary energy, works well. It helps the under-standing of the process if the conclusions from these discussions are portrayed graphically. So, ask each function to display their conclusions on a flip. Using red and blue, it looks a little like a bloodshot eyeball, if you like that kind of thing.

Display these prominently for the remainder of the session (see Figure 2.1).

Now back into the small groups as before, to create descriptions of the nature and quality of the current state of the interactions on the eye, including the health of the personal working relationships. Examples from real sessions are:

- fire fighting and reactive;
- lack of accountability;
- conflicting objectives;
- lack of understanding of each other's processes;
- communication limited to accusations of blame;
- inaccurate information and woolly feedback;
- no one has authority or will to fix things.

Staying in the small groups, have them create descriptions of how these same interactions and relationships should be. Examples from real sessions are:

- based on accurate data;
- timely communication of delivery changes;
- an exchange of accurate, meaningful and reliable information;
- proper agreements on supply arrangements;
- customer needs are anticipated;
- an understanding and acceptance of each other's priorities.

Ask everyone to think about the work they have done over the last few hours, and to bring to next week's session their views on their function's contributions (actual and potential) to achieving agreed objectives, any suggested additions to the eye, and any additions to the description of the current and should-be states.

The process for week 2

To act as a constant reminder of context and purpose, have the unit objectives on the walls – also the eyeball diagrams – although this can give rise to an uneasy feeling of being watched.

Review the experience and output of last week, revisit the objectives and the current and should-be descriptions as required.

In small groups, identify what participants will need to do to close the gap between the current and should-be states. Some of these actions will be quick and simple requiring only one-to-one contracting and some will look big and potentially complex, requiring a more formal and structured negotiating process. Some obviously have much wider implications and a feel of incipient projects. These should be postponed for a few weeks in order for the participants to gain in confidence and practise their new skills on the smaller tasks first.

Report out from the above session in whole group. It is worth doing this more than once. The facilitator should keep an eye on how things are going in the small groups and decide when to call a short plenary. The object is to tie off some conversations and recognize progress in planning for action. This encourages others who are going more slowly and stops people getting bogged down in detail and problems prematurely. It also allows others, who are reticent about contributing, to become engaged and contribute, and is useful for those interactions with wider scope, or those of interest for most of the group.

As these conversations progress, the facilitator should gather brief action plans, write them on flip paper and display them. As the session moves into the last hour, the walls should be covered with many sheets, which will show a subject title, will name those taking responsibility for progress and will show a target completion or review-by date.

Even with the appropriate level of interpersonal skills, it is unrealistic to expect people to succeed without help. The next step is therefore to identify the kind of support required and contract for it. This session involves a lot of noise and many small meetings as people contract with each other for support in taking their initiatives forward. Support can take the form of making time available to talk, lending weight where it is needed, influencing or just staying 'off my back' while I get on with things. It may even mean one person helping out another with some deadlined or other urgent task, like a month-end return, so as to allow them to spend quality time on securing an improvement in their chosen Key Interaction. Creative ways of helping each other should be encouraged. One such meeting, which is best facilitated on the spot, is between the whole group and their Core manager, sometimes also the unit manager(s) of the group(s) present. For this encounter, first ask the participants to produce a set of requests headed, 'To support us best, we need our manager to:

(a) Stop
(b) Start
(c) Do more of
(d) Do less of.'

Examples from real sessions are:

- Stop – excluding us from discussions and decision making – encroaching on (dipping in and out of) our areas of responsibility.
- Start – being more assertive with peers and senior managers – giving us clear definitions of the scope of our authority.
- More of – trust in us to use our initiative – being more available for coaching.
- Less of – constantly and arbitrarily changing priorities.

It is really worth spending a few minutes to record these on flip charts for later distribution, not least because memories fade and perceptions differ.

Where the whole group has an interest, two or three negotiators should be appointed to act as its representatives. Their licence to negotiate on the others' behalf must be explicit, specific and detailed. This is about trust not faith. The Field of Freedom (pp. 101–2) is excellent here. A useful way to keep track of who is doing what and by when is via a responsibility chart. For larger projects this should include an assessment of costs and benefits.

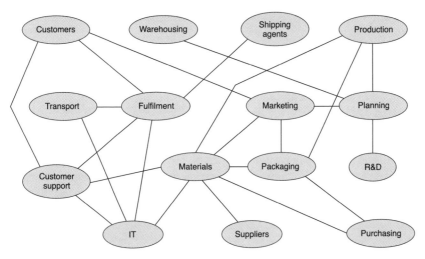

Figure 2.2. The Key Interactions map.

Agree dates and times for the group to meet once again and commit to personal targets to be achieved by then, in a couple of short sentences.

After the round of sessions is complete, it is worth pulling together their output and creating a map of all the interactions which are key to the success of each unit or department involved. This should show Key Interactions within each unit, between each unit and between each element of their department and relevant outside parties including customers. Such a composite map can be useful as a constant reminder to everyone about what is *really* important to the success of the whole operation (see Figure 2.2).

Active management behaviours

This is a composite list from a number of sessions:

- Sharing relevant information, giving well-considered answers to questions, responding positively to challenges, reinforcing messages (e.g. priorities, business directives etc.), using productive language (body, verbal content and tone).
- Seeking out and using information sources, being prepared to ask in the confident expectation that the approach will be treated with respect and not seen as a failing, having the courage to keep asking until there is enough understanding to be confident of success.
- Actively working to understand the fit with the larger operation, what contribution is expected and using initiative to ensure that contribu-

tion is maximized, even when it means moving out beyond traditional boundaries.

- Giving praise for outcomes, for effort and for brave tries, sharing successes generously and spontaneously, being able to say 'I think I did that well'.
- Having the patience and perspective to take a long-term view; having the courage to give up short-term or partisan success for more soundly based long-term performance improvements, which will deliver for the whole organization; anticipating events and problems and taking early action.
- Adopting performance targets and showing this by constantly tracking them through highly visible measures, actively looking for ways to effect improvements in the measures and spontaneously taking action to make them happen even when it crosses a functional boundary.
- Confronting issues that need confronting, never accepting current practice or performance as good enough, showing the courage and will to tackle constructively what is going on, even when such action may meet with opposition, never accepting personal limitations but constantly seeking opportunities to stretch and grow.
- Abandoning traditional practices which no longer reflect business priorities or produce the best results and putting in better ones.
- Giving people clear and specific licence to use their initiative, make decisions and take risks, spending time with others to help them see the big picture, taking time to work with others on what is important to them and helping them maximize their contribution.
- Realistically tracking progress, accepting setbacks and openly learning from them, welcoming and celebrating success, facing up to reality and not trying to hide from it, showing dogged determination and stamina in the struggle to succeed, being prepared to change things in the light of others' contributions and ideas.

Chapter 3

Inspiration and strategy

Social capital is critical to prosperity and to what has come to be called competitiveness.
FRANCIS FUKUYAMA

Most people in big companies today are administered, not led. They are treated like personnel, not people.
ROBERT TOWNSEND

The words leader and leadership are in some danger of becoming a devalued currency. Too much talk not enough real action. Too many titles without the substance to back them up.

Take the title Team Leader, for example. Who can argue with such a wholesome epithet? Teams are good and leading is necessary, so no problem there, we would imagine. Yet, in too many cases those holding the title have little leading to do and are actually responsible for managing a group of people who neither have the characteristics of a single coherent team nor the need to operate like one. Calling someone a Team Leader in these circumstances is a wish statement at best, and at worst, seriously misleading for all concerned. This is symptomatic of a much more general problem.

We believe it is time to tighten up the definitions of leader and manager so that they can both be appreciated for the different contributions they offer to organizations wishing to make progress, particularly those that wish to make progress towards healthier social capital.

In essence, our argument is that while the need to exhibit leadership behaviour exists to varying degrees in most jobs throughout the organization, so too does that other, currently much less fashionable description, managerial behaviour. Rather than vesting spurious and misleading titles on people, it would be better to examine what they should be doing and give these appropriate behaviours, whatever they might be, the prestige and prominence their contribution to the organization's success merits.

By adopting this approach it becomes possible to accept that there are some activities which can properly be described as leadership behaviours and others which can properly be described as managerial. Both are legitimate. Both have positive contributions to make. One is as valuable as the other. They are just different. They provide their value-add in different circumstances and are not the prerogative of any one individual, job, function or level. What *do* vary job by job, function by function, level by level, are the relative proportions of these two valuable ingredients. We refer to this as the mix. Every job-holder must exhibit a different mix of leadership and managerial behaviours if they are to be at their most effective and maximize their contribution to the development of healthier social capital and organizational success.

For those who want to cover the whole range of leadership behaviours, there are already some excellent works around. The recent thinking on Emotional Intelligence, for example, is particularly compatible and we recommend that anyone embarking on the social capital journey should have a full and clear picture of all the leadership behaviours they want and need for their organization. However, our intention in this chapter is to explore only two, both of which are vital to the *early* development of healthier social capital in a successful organization; namely the creation of inspiring Visions and their translation into reality.

From Vision to reality

To be of any use to organizations, a Vision must really be capable of inspiring others. It must engage the hearts and minds and prompt people to put aside petty and partisan ambitions in favour of its fulfilment. It must generate a commitment and a sense of common purpose in those whose strenuous contributions are required to make it a practical reality. It must therefore be communicated in such a way that it is fully understood and bought into by the interested parties who will be required to bring about the necessary transformation.

To be worthy of this degree of commitment, to be credible, a Vision must also have a sound strategy attached. An essential part of the modern leadership tool kit, therefore, must be strategic thinking – the ability to look up and out, to see into the future and spy out the potential opportunities as well as the rocks to be avoided, and not least, the fine judgement to understand what all this might mean in the context of the Vision.

And lastly there is the plan. A Vision without the means to turn it into reality is just wishful thinking, and it is usually a function of modern leadership to provide those means. It is the process of turning inspirational Visions into practical plans that is the subject of most of the rest of this chapter.

In Chapter 1 we introduced the four levels where leadership and management behaviours figure significantly (The Navigator, the Flight Crew, the Core and the Activators). The rationale for choosing these particular titles is explained on p. 8, but they are, respectively, the leader of the organization, the senior managers, the middle managers, and the first-line managers plus a few others who are in non-managerial but influential positions. The following paragraphs take a brief look at how these might be expected to contribute to the creation of Visions and their translation into fact.

The Navigator and the Flight Crew

The Navigator must have a Vision for the organization as a whole. It must be their own too, and not the bland product of a lengthy consultative process. However well they may be crafted, we believe that these committee or consultant generated Visions suffer from a lack of raw energy and the power to inspire when compared to those that spring from a single being. A Vision which does not inspire is a poor useless thing. As it happens we are also rather against an overdependency on Eureka moments whether in or out of baths, preferring for the most part the view that good Visions are the product of some hard thinking, good processes and a proper gestation period.

After the Vision, comes the involvement. It is not enough for the Navigator just to be some kind of ideas machine. Communicating the Vision to others effectively, requires more than just the ability to inspire. The inspired must individually and collectively understand what it is they are engaged upon. The unifying figure in this activity can only be the Navigator who must be willing and able to devote quality time so that everyone, and the Flight Crew in particular, understand the Vision and their role in its realization. This is a key area of the Navigator's contribution which may take a sizeable amount of their time. The investment is essential however and will repay the effort and attention it is accorded. If the Flight Crew are divided or half-hearted, as we have sometimes seen, the journey will be a long and joyless one, with little good at the end of it.

Having secured the hearts and minds of the Flight Crew, they can now be enlisted in actively driving towards the realization of the Vision, and, in this context, healthier social capital. It is essential that those at the top of any organization are in control of events as they unfold. They are the ones who must have the strategic overview and be constantly alert to what is happening or about to happen inside and outside the organization. Specifically their key tasks are:

- developing strategy;
- ensuring the integration and timing of developments into a coherent whole;
- ensuring that resources are brought fully to bear in order to maintain the momentum of the journey;
- actively sensing what is going on;
- planning next steps;
- directing and co-ordinating action across the organization;
- communicating with managers at all levels to ensure that their plans are aligned with the bigger corporate picture;
- recognizing effort and success of those engaged in the struggle;
- constantly providing positive reinforcement for good behaviour;
- providing a ready source of role models (see Chapter 4);
- acting as disciples, ambassadors and champions of the new ways of working.

This represents a major investment of time and energy, which will only be sustained if the return on that investment, namely the journey towards enhanced performance through healthier social capital, is really understood and valued by everyone in these high-level positions.

The Core managers and the Activators

While we would expect to see a majority of *managerial* behaviours from the Core and the Activators as they go about their daily business, we would also expect to see some leadership ones in there as well. If they are to really engage their people and tap into the wealth of talent and energy that exists there, they will need to create Visions for their own areas of responsibility and immediate interest, to inspire others, to think strategically and to make effective plans, as well as excelling in their dominant managerial role of coach and influencer. Of necessity their Visions must be smaller in scale and aligned to the overall Vision, but that in no way diminishes their power or their potential contribution to the general well-being of the organization.

There is one major difference however. Whereas the Navigator has a ready-made Flight Crew to help with the translation of the organization-wide Vision into practical reality, everyone else must find their own supporters. We call these the Planning Groups. They are described later on pp. 67–8 and form a part of 'Planning to Win' – a process for everyone.

The following checklist focuses on the issues raised in this chapter so far and is offered as an aid to checking their relevance to your organization. Try it now or come back later as you feel appropriate.

Checklist

In my organization:

There is a clear and inspiring organization-wide Vision for the future which is widely understood and accepted.   I Agree/I Disagree

There is clear behavioural evidence to support the view that the Flight Crew understand and have bought into that Vision.   I Agree/I Disagree

The Flight Crew know the *individual* contribution they are expected to make to the fulfilment of that Vision.   I Agree/I Disagree

The Flight Crew know the *collective* contribution they are expected to make to the fulfilment of that Vision.   I Agree/I Disagree

The Flight Crew have Visions for their own units which are compatible with the overall vision.   I Agree/I Disagree

The Navigator and the Flight Crew are very active in promoting these high-level visions and can be seen making strenuous efforts personally to adopt the behaviours which are required to support them and develop healthier social capital.   I Agree/I Disagree

The Core managers and Activators are actively encouraged to produce their own visions for their areas of responsibility.   I Agree/I Disagree

Strategic thinking and planning takes place at all levels.   I Agree/I Disagree

People all through the organization understand the contribution that their role is expected to make to the achievement of the whole.   I Agree/I Disagree

If you answered Disagree or perhaps wished there was a 'maybe' category, then your organization may find the Planning to Win process helpful on the journey to healthier social capital and enhanced performance.

Planning to Win

There is a natural and understandable fear that if everyone starts thinking strategically and implementing the plans that result, there will be chaos with a lot of conflicting strategies pulling in different directions and achieving nothing. The dilemma is however, that if organizations are to build healthy social capital and succeed in a challenging and ever-changing environment, then they will need everyone at every level to contribute all their energies, knowledge and talents *including* strategic thinking and planning.

The process we offer to bring this about is simple and we call it 'Planning to Win'. The winners in this case are:

- The organization, which wins short, medium and long term, and does so because its ideas are sharper and more tightly concentrated on delivering the goods, because its people know that their thoughts and opinions really matter, because as a result it attracts and retains higher quality more committed people, and because it consistently places its resources wholeheartedly behind its strategies.
- Individuals and groups within the organization who know they are winners because they are treated as a valued part of a tight, efficient and successful outfit.

What Planning to Win is *not* about is partisan or personal victories over others in the community of interest that is your organization; no faction fights, no politics. Even the much lauded win/win isn't the most desirable outcome in this context. In developing performance through healthier social capital, the best 'win' is the one which benefits the whole organization. Chapter 6 has some more thoughts on this.

There are three principles essential to Planning To Win which are best explained before we describe the process. These are Sustainable Competitive Advantage (SCA), Sustainable Value-add (SV-a) and the importance of marketing.

SCA essentially relates to any edge that the organization either has or could secure reasonably quickly that competitors have not got or could not get for some time. It is relevant for the organization as a whole and for *some* of the key activities within it. Being successful and staying successful demands constant vigilance and not a little opportunism. If there is a chance of a unique trading position it usually has to be seized upon quickly or lost. Only a lucky few who have the patent on some fantastic piece of equipment or unique image can afford any relaxation and even that can be dangerous. On the grand scale, for example, The Walt Disney Corporation have those most durable of SCAs, Mickey Mouse and Donald Duck, and even they might be well advised not to relax too much. For most organizations, however, any competitive advantage is likely to be more transient, lasting only until the competition catch on and develop something similar or better of their own. How much time there is before this happens will vary, but with the good times increasingly prone to a short shelf-life, it is essential that everyone is constantly on the alert for the next winning idea to incorporate into their strategic plans. SCA should be so positioned as to act as a constant reminder.

SV-a on the other hand is about maximizing the contribution that those parts of the organization not in direct competition with the outside world can make to supporting their colleagues who are actively engaged in securing and maintaining the organization's SCA. To achieve this, it is essential that they too make their own strategic plans.

The many support functions in the organization are vital to its success. Without them, those who carry direct responsibility for generating the organization's business, whatever it might be, are unlikely to be able to deliver their SCA. The contribution required of the support functions is to add value to that effort, and in so doing, increase the chances of corporate success. Support functions must therefore look at themselves and the environment in which they operate; they must analyse their strengths and weaknesses; they must look for the opportunities that are possible and the threats they must face. Having done so, they should then be able to identify what they have that no one else in the organization has or could get, their unique contribution which would enable them to provide maximum SV-a to those they support.

An excellent test of the health of any community is the degree to which its people work together effectively and produce results that ensure a successful present and future for the whole venture. A healthy environment demands that people in one unit say to themselves, 'How best can we con-tribute to the work of the other units we support to enable them to succeed and prosper?'

SCA and SV-a are of primary importance, but they will only achieve maximum impact if they are energetically and enthusiastically marketed.

Promoting a SCA through advertising and marketing may seem obvious, but, as the example later in this chapter illustrates, there is often scope to do more. Marketing SV-a is less obvious, less instinctive perhaps. However, if a unit has something which no one else in the organization has, or simply has the resources and talent to do a piece of work better than anyone else, then there is a strong argument for making others aware of that fact. In terms of healthy social capital, such a strategy has the potential to satisfy both the self-interest drive and the need to belong. By maximizing the unit's contribution to the common wealth and being seen to do so, their reputation is likely to be enhanced. The people involved will feel good about themselves and each other. They will try harder and have more confidence to take personal risks like being more creative and innovative. They will want to belong to such a prestigious unit.

Perhaps the role of self-publicist requires further comment since in some societies it may be considered more genteel to 'hide one's light under a bushel' than it is to 'blow your own trumpet'. In organizational life however there are few prizes for the former. This suggests that it is not a question of whether SCA or SV-a should be actively marketed, but rather to whom the marketing should be directed and what form it should take.

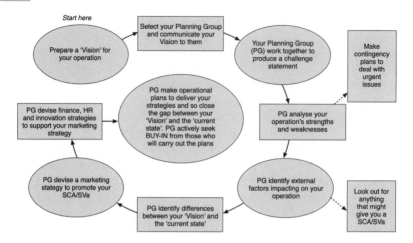

Figure 3.1. The Planning to Win process.

The Planning to Win process

Figure 3.1 shows what the process looks like. Note that the process:

- applies to all levels of management;
- combines Visionary leadership with involvement, consultation and real responsibility;
- focuses strategic thinking and planning on obtaining SCA for the whole organization and SV-a for its constituent parts;
- enables individuals, units and departments to maximize their contributions to the achievements of the whole organization;
- frees up everyone in the organization to become strategic thinkers and planners, tapping its reserves of talent and enlisting them in the pursuit of excellent performance.

The return for investing in Planning to Win

Wherever we work and regardless of organization type or sector, we find people invariably say at some stage that they would produce better results if they spent more time thinking strategically about their role and planning what they could do to maximize their contribution to its success. Yet, in practice, these pursuits remain something of a minority pastime. It seems the daily pressures of modern organizational life are just too heavily weighted in favour of visible action to allow people to make the investment in such an apparently passive process, even when they know it would pay dividends.

Planning to Win helps bring strategic thinking and planning out into the open and makes it a respectable way to spend some quality time. There are four aspects to this:

(a) People at all levels are given licence to think strategically about their area of responsibility, about how they see their department, division or unit in the foreseeable future. They are asked to have a Vision, a strategy and a plan, the only caveat being that these must be so aligned as to enhance the ability of the whole community to deliver on its organization-wide goals.

(b) Cross-functional and multi level involvement is built-in. The process explicitly requires people to come together to help each other with their thinking and planning. It generates an awareness of the real interdependencies which exist in modern organizations and which must work well to ensure collective effectiveness and ultimate success. It also fosters feelings of belonging to something, to a community of interest. People from different functions but with common interests come together, bringing their different skills and perspectives to bear on ideas and issues. Barriers are broken down. Reinforced with good interpersonal behaviours and processes of the kind discussed in Chapters 2, 4 and 6, the conditions are ripe for the development of a sense of community, trust, reputation for reliability and many of the other active ingredients necessary for the development of healthy social capital.

(c) Thinking strategically, planning and turning those plans into reality become just some of the ways the organization does things.

(d) Planning to Win is focused on delivering the tangible and valuable outcomes which will produce visible success. It thus avoids the common planning pitfalls of becoming a self-indulgent, introspective and wasteful, not to say often mind-numbing process.

The process stage by stage

We will now look at each of the stages of the process in more or less the order they naturally occur, although it must be borne in mind that there is something of the iterative in any such activity.

1 Defining Vision

Whatever level in the organization it applies to, Vision is probably best defined by its qualities. It must be clear enough to be understood, but it need not always be very precise. It must be inspiring but not unrealistically ambitious. It must drive all activity and be embodied in clear and achievable goals. It is certainly future orientated, but exactly how far into the future it extends depends very much upon the circumstances, and to some extent on the position of the visionary in question. An unrealizable Vision for a time too far into the future might be vivid, but it is doubtful how many people would deem it worth their while investing time and energy working towards it. Beyond the organization-wide Vision of the Navigator and the large scale ones of the Flight Crew, most are likely to picture a time no more than 2 years in the future and often a good deal less, when things within their sphere of responsibility and interest are operating effectively and efficiently to deliver maximum contribution to the achievement of the organization-wide goals.

2 Developing a Vision

This involves some focused daydreaming – no bath required. Here is one method.

First, imagine it is your habit to keep a diary in which you record everything that happens to you. Then, project yourself into the future to a time when your Vision has been realized. Think of a precise date and imagine yourself sitting down at the end of the day to write up your diary entry. Describe the day at work in detail including significant events, your feelings, how other people behaved and how they reacted to what was going on. It is important that, for the time being, any thoughts about how to change things to achieve this state of affairs are parked. If they are allowed to figure too early in the process, they can be very limiting. But don't lose them. Keep them for later. Instead focus only on the conditions which are likely to be present if your Vision were a reality. The diary entry should now contain the detail of all the constituent parts of your Vision. It is time to rework it into a short story like the one in the box below, which will form the basis of the information you will need to enlist some help with your strategic thinking and planning. It should be challenging but still capable of being achieved within a motivational timescale. Your supporters in this will be your Planning Group (PG).

A manager's Vision story

Early April 2001+... What a day. End of the financial year and the usual rush to produce accounts. My new group performed fantastically though. What a change from a couple of years ago. We worked together to get the job done and the atmosphere was really good. Work is enjoyable again and a real challenge. Being able to select my own people has made such a difference.

We are well on the way to becoming the preferred employer in our area and we are often contacted by others in the industry for comments. I have been told by people from other companies that we are seen as the benchmark for many of our competitors.

I'm so glad I was able to get buy-in to my ideas about creativity and innovation. What a difference that made to the way we do things.

Within a couple of months, I will be leaving this group to join the operation in Europe. I will be taking on much more responsibility but I'm ready for it and I know the boss thinks so too, he told me ... and my group are ready and capable of taking the reins.

You will now need to meet and work with your Planning Group to gain their understanding and acceptance of the Vision story. When they hear it, it should inspire them to want to help. As you need their buy-in, the story must be detailed enough to engage their interest, but not too well worked as to preclude or discourage their input in the form of probing questions, build-ons and suggestions for sharpening up the definition of the Vision. This will not be a rubber stamping exercise. While the Vision is not negotiable, how it might be achieved certainly is. Once this stage is completed you will have an exceptionally powerful driving force at your disposal; a strongly desired, future picture which exerts a pull in its own right, acting both consciously and unconsciously to influence actions and provide a coherence and a common sense of purpose across your activities, and a group of disciples to help you.

3 Translating the Vision into reality

The Planning Group

For the best results, this should comprise three or four people from different disciplines and from different levels. Previous experience is not critically important. In fact, a degree of naivety around the subject is most useful in that it allows people to ask the kind of questions and make the kind of challenges which someone with a bit of background might hesitate to make for fear of looking foolish. The value-add is not unlike that of the 'alien' we suggest you invite to your creativity sessions in Chapter 7. It is not unusual for naive questions to provoke some profound re-thinking.

There is a secondary pay-off as well. The inclusion of unexpected people in the Group puts out a strong signal about social capital and the developing sense of community, of commonwealth, in which the whole is greater than the sum of the parts and everyone has a valued contribution to make. Actions almost always speak louder than words.

The Group's role is to work together to make the Vision a reality, and, while they are not required to do everything themselves, they *will* be responsible for making it happen. For example, returning to the 'manager's Vision' (box on p. 66), they will usually need to tease out in more detail what must happen to translate the Vision into reality. In this instance, they might conclude that the manager should negotiate a deal to allow him more control over the selection of staff, develop his existing people in the skills of working collectively, be a bit more active in marketing himself and his group and so enhance the group's standing with key others inside and outside the organization, provide specific skill and process training and probably contract with his boss for regular support sessions.

The Planning Group need to think strategically and produce sound practical plans based on information gathered from inside and outside the operation. When those plans are complete, they will act as disciples spreading the word, delivering the message throughout the target area and working with key others to secure the buy-in required.

Throughout the planning process, the Group should meet regularly and often. It is sometimes best for the initiator of the Vision to take a role as facilitator so that they do not dominate decisions about implementation, but much depends on the personalities involved. The Group itself should only remain in existence for as long as it takes to produce the plan and secure initial buy-in from key players, after which it must be disbanded. If it isn't, it will just take up valuable time, or worse it will look around for something else to do to justify its continued existence. Be firm. There are usually quite enough aimless committees around already.

Producing a Challenge Statement

The Group should develop a Challenge Statement, based on their recently acquired understanding of the Vision.

A Challenge Statement

Our challenge is that before (date) we will be working together in an environment that is stimulating, enjoyable and productive. We will have little difficulty recruiting high calibre staff as we are considered to be the best employer in the area. Other organizations in our industry will be seeking to use us as a benchmark for how to develop healthy social capital as a means of delivering better and better bottom line results.

A Challenge Statement is the means by which the Vision is communicated throughout the organization (or throughout the area to which the Vision relates). It is a synopsis of the Vision, expressed as a challenge to be achieved. It enables all interested parties to focus their activities by giving them the means to ask themselves, 'Is what I am doing right now going to lead to us meeting our challenge?' The statement should be short, meaningful, easy to remember and designed to motivate, focus and mobilize. It may encapsulate the Vision in its entirety or it may relate to only a part of it, perhaps the current priority. If it refers to only the immediate future, then it follows that further Challenge Statements will be needed as each part is achieved. Either way, it should be reviewed regularly to ensure it remains relevant, and, whatever is decided, it is essential that it is received by those it is targeting as motivational; stretching but achievable. Pies in the sky are always by definition, dangerous confections.

Challenge Statements work best when they are written in plain and concise language avoiding vague, general statements that are open to misinterpretation. As well as stating the challenge, some guidelines for *how* the challenge should be tackled may be included, or simply referred to if they already exist in the shape of organizational value statements and the like.

Identifying the gap

A Vision will only become a reality if the gap can be bridged between where things stand currently and where the Vision says they should be. It is one of the Planning Group's primary tasks to identify the size and nature of that gap.

During this process they must show high levels of self-discipline. They must not become so enthralled with the beauty of the process that they forget that they are there to produce a result, and with some alacrity at that. This happened often in the quality improvement teams of the 1980s, which were referred to with little obvious affection as black holes; they sucked in resources and energy but nothing ever emerged. These often obscure and opaque bodies were also accused of analysis paralysis for the same reason. Another temptation to be avoided, is the emergence of interesting and potentially diverting side alleyways. Their seductive charms can result in all sorts of self-perpetuating behaviour including the Group trying to live forever by widening its remit, or even just rushing off in all directions to 'sort out' the problems they encounter 'while they are there.' The latter is sometimes referred to as action hysteria. To avoid these twin problems the Group must always remain highly focused on the result they have been formed to achieve. Their task is to work themselves out of a job as quickly and efficiently as possible and then go their separate ways.

The first step in bridging the gap between Vision and current reality is to get very clear about the exact nature and scope of that gap. This means a thorough examination of the environments both inside and outside the organization or the unit concerned, as they affect its ability to deliver. As Sun Tzu observes in his 2,500-year-old, but still relevant text, *The Art of War*, 'Know your enemy as you know yourself and in one hundred battles you will not be in peril.' A trifle militaristic and adversarial, perhaps, but the message is apposite enough.

The aim of analysing the environment inside the organization or unit is to obtain a realistic snapshot of the operation uncoloured by any wishful thinking, old scores and hurts or political manoeuvring. Having a mixed, subject-naive Planning Group is particularly helpful in this cause. The purpose in looking outside the immediate boundaries of the organization or unit is to identify threats and opportunities as well as the true state of health of current interactions. However daunting the prospect, however uncomfortable some of the findings may be for fondly held opinions, it is vital to make an objective assessment about where you stand in the wider environment and what factors may affect your prospects for future success.

SWOT analysis has been around a long time, so it probably doesn't need much in the way of an explanation here, and in any case it is always best to tailor the analysis to the specific circumstances. However, the following headings could form a general basis for tackling the analysis. We have grouped these into two sub-categories which relate naturally to SV-a and SCA respectively.

(a) those which apply to the internal interactions between the constituent parts of the organization along with those external interactions which are more collaborative than competitive in nature.
(b) those which relate specifically to the *competitive* position of the organization as a whole and those units which are directly responsible for generating the organization's business, whatever it might be.

INTERNAL/EXTERNAL INTERACTIONS

Stated aims: Are the stated objectives of the particular unit or organization clear to all the people who must deliver them? How are they perceived and is everyone who needs to be, fully committed to their achievement?

Working environment: How close are we to having a sense of community? How well do we work together? How much trust and respect actually exists? How do we handle conflict and different perspectives? Do we give as much weight to enhancing working relationships as we do to task outcomes? Are we collectively effective?

Resources: How well are we using the resources we currently have? Are they integrated and focused on delivering the Vision? If not, why not?

Communication: What is the quality *really* like? Who says so? Are the right people talking to each other? More importantly still, are they listening to each other? Does communication and information exchange flow freely up, down and across, wherever it is required? Are these typically monologues or dialogues?

Leadership and managerial behaviour: How skilled are people in these behaviours? Are they good at selecting the most appropriate ones to fit any circumstance, or do they have only one 'comfortable' style they use for all occasions? Is the critical mass of people working in ways which will deliver healthier social capital and meet the Vision for the unit?

Technical and functional skills: What key skills are required to deliver the Vision and are these present? Do we have them in sufficient quantity?

People: Have we got the right people in the unit? Do we have a really good description of the kind of people we need? Are we helping people to grow into the people we need?

Creativity and innovation: How willing and able are we to take on and seek out new ideas, concepts and ways of working? How often does that apparent willingness translate into action?

Internal and external customer/supplier relationships: Are the interactions of high quality and are they taking us closer to the realization of our Vision? How would we describe the key relationships in this area? How would others describe them? Is our treatment of key others consistent with the development of healthier social capital?

Systems: Do they help or get in the way? Are they outmoded or still appropriate?

Structure: How flexible and responsive is it? Does it help or hinder us in achieving the Vision effectively and efficiently?

Perception and influence: How is the unit perceived by others within the organization, and what is the organization's image on the outside? What effect do these perceptions have on resource allocation, level of influence, effectiveness and success?

Attracting staff: How competitive are our pay rates and benefits packages compared to other employers with whom we compete for staff? How do development opportunities compare? Is our working environment more or less attractive? Are we competing for scarce skills and doing so successfully?

COMPETITIVE POSITION

Competitor financial strength: What is their share price doing? How are their finances geared? How liquid are they? What assets do they have? What is their profit margin?

Competitor products: What new products or services have they recently brought to market? What is their market niche? What is the quality of their products?

Competitor ability/willingness to innovate: Do they invest in research and development? Is their organization structured to be flexible and responsive to change? Are they more or less switched onto future technological developments/opportunities than we are?

Competitor marketing strategy: How do they promote their products and services? What is their profile in the marketplace? How quickly are they moving there?

Customers and demography: What is the age range and income level of our customers? Who are our customers and who aren't they?

Political and economic trends: What is the general political 'complexion' of the environment we need to work in? Could the realization of the Vision be affected by political, legislative or economic changes?

Social trends: How are people spending their leisure time? If spending patterns are relevant, what are they? What are young people doing (music and fashion often give serious clues to society)? Is the so-called grey market relevant?

If there is a need to go into more detail, there are always systems such as Michael Porter's Value Chain Analysis or macro scanning processes like PEST (Political, Economic, Social and Technical) which may be useful.

With this level of investigation, the Planning Group is able to develop a true and objective view of the current position, and, using the Challenge Statement and Vision story for comparison, to identify any gaps which may exist between it and the Vision. Additionally, they are now well placed to begin to generate all sorts of ideas about what will give them an SCA or a SV-a.

Deciding the way forward

The Group can now start to work on the creative process of generating ideas about the best way forward. This is a much less systematic process than gathering and categorizing the data and looks for patterns and connections that are not immediately apparent. The Uccello™ Process described in Chapter 7 can be particularly useful here.

The aim is to find strategies which deliver SCA to the organization as a whole and to the key activities of some functions within it, as well as SV-a for all supporting functions inside the organization. The steps in the process are the same for either.

Devising strategy

The difference between a strategy and a plan is aptly illustrated by the following anecdote. During one of the many Gulf War news briefings, a journalist asked the General, 'What is your strategy for dealing with the enemy?' 'We're going to cut them off and destroy them,' was the reply. 'How are you going to do that?' asked the persistent journalist. 'That's operational,' said the General. From this example, it is clear that a strategy can be defined as what you are going to do and a plan as how you are going to do it.

By definition, therefore, strategy comes first. The broad choices are to develop a strategy based on something you already have (grow), do something different (change) or leave things as they are (no change). The last of these is a legitimate option, but only as long as it is a considered judgement. Within these headings the actual *focus* of any particular strategy will depend on the analysis which has been carried out and the assessment of the Planning Groups as to where the best pay-offs lie.

However, whether dealing with SCA or SV-a, we believe that there is a strong argument for selecting *marketing* as the first strategy to be considered. Where a true advantage or a value-add has been identified, it will need to be promoted vigorously if it is to have maximum impact. As we observed on p. 63, the 'light under a bushel' approach does no-one any favours, and in fact runs counter to the whole concept of 'investing in social capital'. Other strategies will then flow from this, but arguably it is the SCA or SV-a and how these are perceived, that will make the critical difference to the performance of the unit or organization.

Here are two examples from our experience which illustrate the importance of an effective marketing strategy for SCA and SV-a, and for the welfare of the organization as a whole:

SUSTAINABLE COMPETITIVE ADVANTAGE

Some time ago we ran a Planning To Win workshop for one of our clients, after which they devised a strategy which they felt would give them a significant edge over their competitors.

They were, however, slow to market their idea both internally and externally, and, perhaps as a result of the former, the organization failed to allocate the kind of resources which would have been needed to ensure a speedy success in the marketplace.

Recently, we learned that a competitor in that industry had adopted a strategy which sounded virtually identical. We investigated discreetly. It seemed that there had been some cross-border personnel movement. Apparently, a senior manager from our client company, having become disheartened by the continual failure of his organization to make the most of his unit's good ideas, had moved with more than a couple of pens and his favourite desk ornament.

The lesson? If the first organization had resourced their strategy properly then they really would have had a SCA. It could have been marketed aggressively, and would have put them in a strong position, setting them apart from their competitors who would have had some catching up to do. Because they did not market the idea well internally, the organization did not get behind it as they might have. The result? People became frustrated and the opportunity for a competitive edge was lost.

Not only does this example illustrate the importance of SCA to the success of the organization, perhaps even in some extreme cases, its very survival. It also demonstrates the consequences which can result when people feel they are not being given the opportunities to contribute all they could. People who feel part of the organization, who have been involved in the strategic planning process and have bought into the Vision will go out of their way to protect their SCA. People who don't feel that way may take their winning ideas elsewhere, and usually the best people at that.

SUSTAINABLE VALUE-ADD

A client recently recounted how her IT department had resolved a difficulty by identifying and marketing their SV-a. Her unit were a strong and capable group who, in the past, had produced some excellent work.

However their morale and self-confidence were low, largely as a result of feeling unappreciated by anyone outside the immediate group. There was a strong feeling that many of their innovations did not have the wide impact they deserved and people were becoming frustrated. There was a danger that some of the best ones would start looking elsewhere for their job satisfaction, and they might not have all that far to look. Another IT department, elsewhere in the organization, were regularly accorded the accolade of 'best in company' even though our client's group had produced at least as many new ideas and despite on occasion their having contributed valuable improvements to the other department's ideas and initiatives. There was no real hostility between the groups, therefore, but something had to be done.

Our client had a clear picture of what she wanted; a happy unit working enthusiastically to produce the innovative solutions she knew they were capable of. She also knew that this was not going to happen unless her department got some recognition from the wider organization. She could see they needed to develop much stronger relationships with their key customers and suppliers and at the same time to increase their profile throughout the organization.

Working together, the unit identified everything they might offer to provide added value to their internal customers. For example, they had the skills to give quick and effective problem-solving support and the capability of providing a 'minimum down-time' commitment to ensure their customers were never without the technology they needed to do their work. They also agreed to meet regularly and often with their customers to identify any problems and find out specific needs so that systems could be tailored to suit. Our client then arranged for an article in the company magazine to be written about the initiatives which included endorsements from their internal customers and photographs of the proud unit – a bold move at a time of some psychological fragility!

Nowadays, they work with their customers to evaluate the impact of changes and developments that have been made and their conclusions appear in an on-line 'information bank'. As a result, both customers and providers feel more in tune with each other. The higher profile and closer working relationships have both increased productivity and enhanced people's sense of personal and professional worth dramatically.

We believe that these examples demonstrate why marketing should be considered as a natural first choice strategy, regardless of whether the specific initiative it is supporting involves growing, changing or staying the same. If an organization and the people in it are going to be winners, this will be accomplished more quickly and more comprehensively if they are not only good at what they do but are appreciated for their positive qualities both in and outside the organization.

Some of the other areas from which strategies may spring include finance, human resources, customer and supplier relations, systems and technical improvements. Circumstances vary and so too does the relative importance of each of these for any given unit or organization. However, we would single out one other for particular comment here. Our experience suggests that strategies for *innovation* frequently rank amongst the most important. They have relevance in virtually every area of work and often make the difference between success and failure in an ever-changing environment.

Making plans

Recalling the Gulf War example, the Planning Group now need to get involved in the practicalities of 'how' and plan the steps that will be needed to deliver the selected strategy. Plans may be simple or complex, but they must be specific. They must specify exactly who is responsible for carrying them out and include performance measures and target dates for completion. This may be stating the obvious, but it is surprising how many woolly, vague plans still see the light of day. Sadly, that is often all they see.

Getting buy-in

The reason most plans fail is because of a lack of buy-in. All too often, plans are introduced with a loud fanfare and are hailed (by their authors at least) as the next great initiative, only to be treated with anything from a kind of hysterical and glassy-eyed enthusiasm, through politically cynical support, to apathy and disdain by those who are supposed to implement them. Though some of these reactions may spring from what is variously known as initiative fatigue or 'death by a thousand initiatives' amongst the troops, this is a secondary reaction. The primary cause is failure to get buy-in.

It need not happen. If the Planning Group has been selected from a cross-section of the workforce, then the conditions will be right for a high level of involvement at every stage, the only exception being the creation of the Vision itself. The Group should involve others from the start. Their working must be transparent to all. Every opportunity should be taken to enlist others in the activities needed to complete the plan, analysing the current state being just one example. The Group must work actively to share information as the plan develops and show people that any contribution they make is recognized, valued, and, wherever possible, adopted.

Our experience is that when people are consistently involved from the beginning and offered a genuine part to play, they become enthusiastic partners who spontaneously act to spread the good word. Others see the advantages and start to form Planning Groups of their own and there develops a critical mass of people who feel engaged and involved. When practical and observable successes start to spring from the resultant plans, even more people get involved and another step towards better bottom lines and healthier social capital is accomplished.

Planning to Win is founded on the three principles:

1   Sustainable Competitive Advantage, which requires the organization to constantly seek out and maximize any unique trading position, however temporary;

2   Sustainable Value-add, which requires support functions to identify and maximize whatever unique contributions they may have to offer the organizational commonwealth; and

3   the need for both to be marketed effectively.

It is a simple process, but one which incorporates all the integrative elements so essential to the development of a sense of belonging and ultimately a healthier social capital.

The following checklist focuses on the Planning To Win process and is offered as an aid to checking its relevance to your organization and the specific ways of working that currently exist. Try it now or come back later as you feel appropriate.

Checklist

In my organization:

People at all levels develop visions of how they see their area of responsibility in the future and take appropriate action to turn them into reality.	I Agree/I Disagree
Peoples' visions are always aligned with a known corporate aim.	I Agree/I Disagree
Planning Groups include a cross-section of people from a number of levels and parts of the organization.	I Agree/I Disagree

During the planning process people who will be affected are actively encouraged to contribute.	I Agree/I Disagree
The process is transparent, information is shared throughout and responses are really listened to.	I Agree/I Disagree
Relevant and realistic Challenge Statements exist even if they are not called that.	I Agree/I Disagree
Strategic plans reflect a thorough analysis of any internal and external factors that may materially affect their translation into reality.	I Agree/I Disagree
Plans are always clear and specific about who will do what and when.	I Agree/I Disagree
We give strategic thinking and planning the right amount of time and energy, neither getting bogged down nor rushing too quickly to a solution.	I Agree/I Disagree
We are constantly vigilant and analyse areas of responsibility at least annually.	I Agree/I Disagree
Analysis of the external environment is at least as thorough as the internal.	I Agree/I Disagree
We consciously and consistently seek out what will give us SCA or SV-a as appropriate.	I Agree/I Disagree
All strategies are determined by what we need to do to promote our SCA or SV-a.	I Agree/I Disagree

If you answered Disagree or perhaps wished there was a 'maybe' category, then your organization may find the Planning to Win process helpful on the journey to healthier social capital and enhanced performance.

Chapter 4

Of hearts and minds and associated body parts

With a particular focus on middle and senior managers

> *Whatever his personal indulgence,*
> *his theology had always been unimpeachable.*
> EVELYN WAUGH OF A POOR ROLE MODEL

> *If there are two ends there is always a middle – and it tends to be*
> *in the centre of things*
> ANON.

When it comes to creating new social capital, all managers should be engaged. Indeed the ideal, pretty well unrealizable in all but the smallest organizations, is for every person regardless of their position to be actively involved in driving the change – always allowing that their specific contributions and the direct focus of their attention will vary with the function and level they occupy.

Yet in practice, getting anything like that degree of engagement is not easy, and one sector in particular seems almost always to produce more than its fair share of problems – middle management, or, as we have chosen to refer to it in this book, Core management. In one multinational we know, problematic Core managers are referred to as the damp proof course. For those readers like ourselves without building credentials, we believe the implication is that nothing will pass through. Not all Core managers fall into this definition of course. It is always possible to find enlightened people within their ranks, who epitomise the positive qualities and behaviours which are discussed later in this chapter and in Chapter 6, but there are usually more than enough of the other kind too.

This presents a real challenge for the Navigator and their Flight Crew, because, when it comes to implementing change and establishing healthy social capital, Core managers represent the single most important group in the organization.

Why are they so important? Perhaps a good way to illustrate this is to recall a conversation with a client, which took place some time into a Key Interactions initiative (see Chapter 2), when things had reached a tricky stage. The vehicular analogy which follows is by no means new, but it worked well then, so here goes.

The client himself was the true visionary leader of the initiative, but because his division was, despite its central and critical role, a small one (120+ managers and staff), he was also his own Flight Crew. The dual nature of the role made it all the more demanding but he was up to it. As Navigator, he was clear about the direction he wanted to take, he had energy and enthusiasm, he had spent time trying to make sure that everyone understood the destination, and, just as important, what the journey would be like. As his own Flight Crew he was responsible also for driving the strategy and creating momentum. He was aware of this and accordingly had carried out his driverly duties with some assiduity. He had made sure the means to move the vehicle were present in the shape of time and resources. He was doing everything he could to support the initiative, including trying to be a role model and sometimes failing. (People like the occasional failure in a role model, as long as it is not too serious and is followed by some kind of repentance.) Anyway, the long and the short of it was that he was pressing the accelerator and he could hear the engine revs rising.

His people on the ground, the engine if you like, (the operators, specialist, technical and administrative staff, along with the first line managers whom we call Activators in this book) all, well almost all, seemed to be doing the new things they needed to do to turn the vision into reality. Yet progress was not as fast or dramatic as it should have been for all that effort and commitment. With the engine roaring like that, the scenery should have been going by in a blur and it wasn't. Something was preventing all that energy and enthusiasm turning into major progress.

Like all good mechanics we did our diagnostics. There were some small technical improvements which could be made, but the main problem was clear. The clutch was slipping. Worse. Some people had not even engaged forward gear yet. Something about time and other priorities? There may even have been the odd surreptitious foot lingering near a brake pedal. Core management was resisting. Undramatically, and often with the *appearance* of acceptance, some Core managers were quietly dragging their heels, or, if you prefer to prolong the vehicular analogy, pulling on the hand brake while the driver was looking the other way. What they were not engaged in doing was putting the engine in gear and letting out the clutch. Ever felt that inexplicable drag on one of your initiatives or projects?

'But, surely' you may say, 'resistance is something we have to contend with at all levels! What is so special about Core management?' And your interjection is far from unjustified and your question is a good one. In order to answer it we must first direct our attention towards hierarchy. If the problem with really engaging the whole organization in a new way lies so often in the middle of the hierarchy, why not cut it out as far as we can. Indeed, that is what many organizations in the 1980s and 1990s did, though not always precisely for that reason. Hence, while we still have hierarchies, they are for the most part much flatter, on paper at least.

The flaw with this concept is that, if there is a role for a number of people whose patch of direct responsibility lies somewhere between organization-wide and a single operational group, then they are probably acting as Core managers regardless of what you call them. The term is effectively defined by the role. Core managers are managers who find themselves in the middle and that feeling of middle exists just as much within a flatter organization as it did before – perhaps even more so, as the function is squeezed and exposed to increasing amounts of challenge and accountability. Often, Core managers in modern, flatter organizations resemble a small nation state buffered between two large and aggressive neighbours, and experience similar levels of discomfort and trepidation.

There is another reason why hierarchy will not go away entirely and this takes us back to a theme we have explored in Chapter 1. It is that hierarchy seems to meet some kind of basic human need. True, some may prefer the view from the top, rather than having to crane their necks to see what the Gods on Olympus are about, but not everyone takes this view by any means. There can be something secure and comforting about knowing one's place, even though it may not be fashionable to say so. The otherwise talented and valuable individual, who knows that s/he is always best as number two, is an example. Others may value hierarchy as a means of mitigating the risk and responsibility. For a graphic demonstration of this in action, try being a fly on the wall at some team briefings. Listen to managers who are not engaged, using words like, 'Management say ...' 'The brief says ...' Even if they don't say the words, everyone gets the message between the lines and in the body language. Ownership can be tough and those above are fair game to blame.

So, if we can agree that Core management *will* persist as a role in spite of any attempts to eliminate it from the organization chart, then it is probably worth taking a closer look at its potential for positive and negative impact on an organization's ability to achieve the goal of healthier social capital.

The cast of players

There are many characters in the cast of core management. It is not necessarily a function of age or length of employment. It could even be argued that it is as much a state of mind as anything. There are those pausing briefly on the stairway to the stars, of course. There are singletons who are regarded as Core managers because of some rare and arcane expertise. There are some who have reached their peak or even gone a bit beyond it. There are the stymied and frustrated CEOs-in-waiting. There are the mentally retired or just tired. There are those who have accumulated vast experience and knowledge but who are perfectly in tune with change and contribute their wealth freely to others. There are the cave dwellers who worship the gods of days gone by, even clinging nostalgically to old titles and terminologies. There are those who relate all present experiences to some golden past of their own. There are those who have reached a level with which they are content and who have made their rightful choice to see work as only one facet of their lives. Each will play their part. The way they interpret it and the conviction they give it, is often dependent on how they are treated.

The role of Core manager

Is it possible to cast Core managers, as a group, as leaders of a climate change on the scale of developing social capital? A sobering thought, perhaps, and one which we believe also runs the risk of diverting attention away from the area in which they have the potential to make their greatest contribution. In fact, that potential contribution lies less in leading, which for them should occupy only a relatively small, but still important portion of their time, and more in managing. All the processes in this book require Core managers to be proficient in the management skills of coaching and facilitation, for instance, and to use them for a large proportion of their daily business. The nature of this new management role is described in more detail in Chapters 3 and 6 and is vital to the development of healthier social capital.

The potential contribution

The key to utilizing this powerful resource and realizing its positive potential lies in the degree to which the individuals concerned are prepared to let go of their old roles and embrace the new. If persuaded, they can place a positive interpretation on anything coming from above. They can be energetic ambassadors. They can be troubleshooters. They can bring a practicality to strategic initiatives. They can take slightly-off ideas and make them work. They can challenge and confront. They can help break down boundaries which exist in the minds of their people and use their credibility to tackle peers who are less convinced. With these guys on the case you have powerful allies.

What then, might prevent that potential from being realized? Why *would* Core managers oppose change, particularly this kind of change, when it offers the opportunity for them to have such an impact on the future of the organization? Well, in fact, when you think about it in terms of human self-interest, resistance is much easier to understand than zeal in this context. These are successful people and their success has been built on certain ways of operating. They are good at them and they are comfortable with them or at least more comfortable than they would be embarking on new ones. And, in addition to the discomfort factor, there is the assessment of the personal risk involved in actively engaging in the proposed change. This may be conscious or unconscious, explicitly raised by the Core manager or only detectable by reading between the lines of their behaviour, but why should they take the risk of trying something new if they can get away with not doing it? It can, of course, be argued with some justification, that there is also a risk in standing still, but this argument is much less psychologically attractive when the change is initiated by others. Furthermore, such an argument may not stack up with their own recent experience. They may well be able to cite other high-profile initiatives which have gone the way of all flesh, sometimes taking their champions and acolytes with them. A wait-and-see policy may commend itself even to those who have some sympathy with the new route intended.

Factors that make Core managers special

Position and proximity

Their central position in the organization structure makes them ideally placed to exert an influence, positive or negative. They are usually in daily contact with other managers and staff and so the sheer number of contacts means they have impact. How they make use of these opportunities is key to the development of social capital, particularly in its vulnerable early growth stages, but also later when their help is needed to assist their people in crossing difficult functional boundaries, tackling status clashes in project groups and so on.

Power over present and future well-being

Core managers also have a strong hierarchical power. Their stars may not burn as brightly as those of the Gods on Olympus but their whims, wraths and preferences have significantly more impact on the day-to-day lives of those who work for them. If it is a straight choice between pleasing one of the remote great ones or the immediate boss, the sensible player hesitates for hardly a moment. The person with the power over their immediate welfare and foreseeable future success is rarely a senior manager. It is almost always the Core manager and all do well to remember that. Who is it that gives out the dirty jobs, those 'special projects', for instance, which can be a passport to either fame or oblivion? Who is it that decides whether to allocate the high performing staff to your unit or steers the troublemakers, the walking wounded and the barely breathing your way? Backing the big boss against the Core manager has been done of course, but it is not a low-risk strategy and is probably only for those who are highly ambitious, mobile or with private fortunes of their own; and there we have it. Power to alter the destinies of others is a function of position and role in the hierarchy of the community, and, by definition, Core managers occupy a position of very special influence. In their command of business strategy, in the scope of their decisions and the consequences of their judgements, the reach of Core managers may bear no comparison to the Navigator or Flight Crew. Yet in their ability to impact on the attitude of whole regiments of others toward change, the Core manager has few equals.

The knowledge and experience pool

Core managers often represent the greatest available pool of experience and knowledge within an organization. Of course while some of it is still valuable, some will inevitably have passed its sell-by date. However, the assessment of what is still valuable and what is not, is a subjective one with perceptions differing quite dramatically, and some of those perceptions have a significant emotional investment behind them. If they can be persuaded to contribute the former while letting go of the latter without rancour, then Core managers can be real assets in engaging the organization's resources to achieve the vision.

The potential barriers

An objective analysis reveals that, of all the groups involved, Core managers can easily see themselves as having the most to lose and the least to gain; and yet what is needed is their wholehearted support. This can only be achieved by the Navigator and Flight Crew recognizing what issues may have negative potential and addressing them appropriately. Here are some examples, along with some thoughts about ways of tackling them which might win hearts and minds to the cause.

Traditional power and status

Many Core managers have built power and status through their command of tasks and technical aspects of the work. They see the value of that contribution in real decisions and action and can offer factual evidence to support their value-add. They like this! The action is direct and the results measurable. This does not seem to compare favourably with many of the new ways, such as coaching people to think for themselves, described in Chapter 6 which can feel at first like a rather second-hand contact with reality. It seems to lack the immediacy of the high that comes from swift and sure decisive action – so good for the personal feel-good factor and the self-image.

Why should they give up the security of hard won power and status for the uncertainty of a new set of skills which they may not be so good at? And even if they *can* perform well, will it be as rewarding? Will it be as exciting?

Suggested action: The new role must be made to feel as exciting and stimulating as the old one. Recognition and rewards for new behaviours, delivered hard on the behaviours themselves, can help condition the Core managers to enjoy the new ways.

Writing off the past

'Why should I?' questions *can* be simply a request for information, but they can also be an indicator of high levels of stress, anger, anxiety or deep hostility. Amongst longer serving Core managers facing radical change, for example, feelings of insult and even outrage are not uncommon. These often spring from a sense, justified or otherwise, that they are being told that they have been doing the job all wrong till now. In extreme cases this can feel like they are being asked to deny the worth of much of their lives. If the Flight Crew is lucky, they may be asked something like, 'Are you saying I have been wasting my time for years – doing it all wrong, and now you have come along to tell me how to do it right?' In that event at least the issue is out in the open and can be addressed even if the process is painful and time consuming. However, these sentiments are more usually kept concealed, only to surface as unpredictable responses and apparently inappropriate displays of anger or aggression. Not good and not easy to deal with.

Suggested action: These explosive sentiments can be most surprising for the Flight Crew to handle. They do not sit well with the common Core manager image of robust toughness. There is therefore a strong tendency, not to say temptation, to take the 'Why should I' question at face value, and, as a result, to treat the symptoms instead of the root cause. This is rarely a productive strategy, although it may seem to save time in the short term. If the Core manager concerned is truly an ally worth having, then the Flight Crew must probe below the superficial, get to the real reasons and deal with them. They must openly consider the 'Why should I?' question from the Core manager's standpoint. If this sounds soft and touchy feely, it doesn't usually feel that way in practice. Ways of doing this are discussed in more detail in Chapter 6.

Tunnel vision

All too often it is the new that gets almost all the positive Flight Crew attention, whether it be new people, ideas, systems, knowledge or ways of working. The implicit message is not lost on those whose credentials may have been built up over time. They rightly deduce, consciously or unconsciously, that people, in this case their bosses, usually like to direct their attention, energy and time toward those things that they regard as important and of relatively high value. It is but a small step to the conclusion that the opposite is also true. Little attention means little perceived value.

When Core managers start to draw this kind of conclusion about how they are viewed, there is trouble in the air for any new initiative, and that is not the end of the problem. Those who feel they may have grounds to take offence, are often the most alert for further corroborative evidence with which to confirm their feelings. Explicit words and thoughtless deeds by those above often tend to reinforce the Core managers' sense that they are not appreciated, fuelling the fires of grievance and resentment all too easily.

Suggested action: Navigator and Flight Crew would do well to treat Core managers' perceptions as both real and significant, even when they are wrong. They must put as much time and energy as possible into explicitly valuing the knowledge, experience and long-held skills which they consider are still relevant. Even mature plants need feeding and watering and some positive vibes in order to flower.

Being stuck with a label

Labelling comes in many forms, like *The Old Guard*, or *Dinosaurs,* or *Difficult* or *Worth Watching*. It is a form of shorthand, a caricature, and that is what makes it at once so convenient and so problematic.

The problem is that any label worthy of the name is sticky and usually too short and snappy to be much use as a comprehensive description of the article in question. That may or may not be fine for a can of beans, but in relations at work it can have a very destructive side, not least in the kind of responses provoked in the labelled.

Labelling need not even be conscious or spoken. The thoughtless deeds we referred to above are just as powerful, especially so when people are perhaps feeling a trifle insecure or threatened. The danger is that, in these circumstances, Core managers perceive that they are being accorded a no- or low-value label and decide to do something about it.

That could take the form of a conscious decision to raise the issue with the boss and clear the air, but usually it doesn't. Most response strategies are much less productive. One of these is the self-fulfilling prophecy. The rationale would go something like this, although in truth it is rarely expressed. 'If I cannot overturn an unreasonable, illusive or personally threatening view about me, then I might as well give them what they expect.' Thus the labeller gets the response they expect and their view is reinforced. Small satisfaction if the label is a negative one, of course.

More serious still is the situation which occurs when those who perceive they have a no- or low-value label come to believe it. There is strong evidence to suggest that negative labels placed on school children in their early years by teachers are very persistent throughout later life, even in the face of considerable evidence to the contrary. Are we so mature that we are immune to them in later life? The authors have certainly met senior managers who act as though they believe this, and one who more or less said so.

Other possible responses include malicious obedience (doing what the organization demands while knowing the folly of the particular action) and of course sabotage, which is more common than any of us would like to think. It may be, of course, that a few of these successful and high status people are prepared to empty their desks and go quietly to their gardens without extracting some compensation on the way. Alternatively, others may choose to stick around to undermine the credibility of future initiatives, something which they are ideally placed to do.

Suggested action: Navigator and Flight Crew must make a conscious and strenuous effort to treat people in ways which emphasize their importance to the future of the organization. In times of change, these ways must be conspicuous and repeated frequently. If certain individuals have no contribution to make, they should be gone, but no labels please.

Fear of failing and something much worse

'What if the skills are too difficult and I have no aptitude for the new role? What if those young graduates and those articulate operators are better than I am? What will become of the power and status it has taken so much time and effort to win over the years? What will they think of me when they see me fail? And worst of all, how will I feel about myself?'

Suggested action: These very human doubts and fears are rarely volunteered, which makes them all the more difficult to address. The Flight Crew must be able to (a) convince Core managers that it is in their interests to let go of some of the skills, behaviours and knowledge which have taken them to a level of success in the past, and (b) show them how they can maintain and enhance their self-esteem and standing while they do it. One approach, which allows Core managers to build up new skills outside the glare of the spotlight, is discussed in Chapter 5 (pp. 99, 124, 127 and 130) in the context of developing the Activators. The principle is applicable to any new skill or behaviour and particularly to the role of coach and facilitator.

The feel of being in control

Control and the fear of losing it, figure highly in the minds of many during major change, and Core managers are no exception. 'Why should I give up control in favour of influence, as this new role in social capital demands? Because that is what you are asking me to do, when I start coaching and facilitating, isn't it? How will I keep a grip on developing events and what my people are doing, if I spend a large proportion of my time coaching and most of the rest of it thinking strategically or trouble shooting across boundaries, as you suggest? How will people know I am the boss then?'

Suggested action: Senior managers must work hard to show Core managers that the new role they are taking on has as much or more to offer in terms of status and satisfaction as its high-control predecessor.

Telltale behaviours to watch out for

The negative potential of Core managers lies in the degree to which they are not prepared to let go of their old roles and embrace the new and occurs for the most part when they don't feel a part of a change which they regard as imposed and not in their interests. When they feel that way, they have the power to kill most initiatives and sometimes the organization too and some of the following behaviours may be observed.

The shimmy

With little more than a few non-verbals, Core managers can give out the clear signal that this new stuff is not something people should be expending too much energy on. Subtly changing the subject a couple of times when enthusiastic junior managers and staff raise the topic works quite well too. The message is that anyone who is so insensitive as to be unable to read my subtle signals about this unworthy project or scheme will only progress in this organization over my dead body. Almost never said outright, of course, but most people would recognize the deal.

The dabble

Dabbling is also quite effective in putting the skids under new behaviours still in their infancy. This involves asking how things are going (good) and then taking over bits of the task (bad) and then not doing them (very bad).

The block

When subtle messages fail to produce the desired effect, the Core manager must get a bit more overt. 'Don't do this. It is not your role. This is more important. And anyway, "the boss" simply wouldn't like it if you approach him direct.' Smacks a bit of sabotage? Perhaps, but try tackling the experienced Core manager about it. The injured innocence is often worthy of an award and the counter arguments quite convincing: and while you tackle the manager, you might give a thought to what awaits any poor whistle-blowers when you have gone.

The spanner

Hardly worth a mention really. Not because it doesn't work but because it is so-o-o-o simple. A well placed spanner has always had a very interesting effect on moving machinery. A word in the wrong place, a piece of information withheld – so many to choose from.

Passive resistance

The task is received and apparently understood. Wheels appear to be in motion and the engine is making lots of noise, but there is no progress. Lack of resources, boss. Other priorities. Had to take George off and put him onto that other job – and so on.

To summarize

Whilst the Navigator is of paramount importance in generating the vision of a way forward which inspires, and the Flight Crew, their disciples, are responsible for creating strategic momentum, it is the Core managers who are frequently the difference between a good idea and a practical reality, between success and failure.

This group, often viewed as an impediment to change, are in fact the most overlooked and undervalued asset when it comes to engaging an organization's resources in delivering change – or not as the case may be!

Within their ranks there will be some who embrace the new ways wholeheartedly. If you have been able to select your own and have done so cleverly, then most of your Core managers will be like this. However, if you have inherited most of your people as many managers do, then you may have a much more mixed bag.

Core managers are uniquely well placed and equipped to provide timely support for the fragile new ways when confidence is low, when setbacks look bigger than they are and when the siren-calls of the old ways beckon with their seductive offer of familiar comfort. Beyond the early stages they have the experience to provide the continuity, meaning and context essential to embed the new ways in sometimes hostile soil and the clout to deal with any problems that arise, such as attacks by any, as yet unreconstructed, members of their peer group.

In practice it is a question of critical mass – engaging enough of these key people to effectively create healthier social capital.

A way forward

Organizations wishing to embark on this journey toward healthier social capital and all the benefits it offers, must act in the following ways to ensure that most Core managers feel themselves in tune with the objective:

1   Organizations must work to identify and meet both the self-interests of Core managers and their need to belong in the new community. If the fact that the route to community lies through the satisfaction of individual self-interests is a paradox, then it is a very human one.

If self-interest is not addressed, if something of real value is not offered in exchange for their commitment to the cause, then managers will inevitably revert to old tried and tested behaviours which have served them well in the past. Too often, the deal they are offered is the opportunity to give up control, accept a drop in status, lose face and to deny the value of skills that have served them well for years. It is hardly surprising that many gracefully decline.

It should be so obvious as to be unworthy of comment, but champions of change must work constantly to ensure that the new package is at least as attractive as the old one.

2   In particular, the new replacement role must be at least as high *status* as the old one, so that Core managers feel it is worth their while to:

- become coaches and facilitators, focusing their attention on a concerted and coherent objective which they have bought into and which they understand will enhance their standing despite its unfamiliarity and consequent associated discomfort.
- become strategists in their own fields who use their position to see further and to help those who work for them to look up and out.
- become skilled in a range of leadership behaviours themselves, able to select and apply different styles as appropriate to meet situational variables.
- acquire, or start to apply more, the level of sensitivity and interpersonal skills necessary to be able to handle excesses of enthusiasm and pursuits of hobby horses up blind alleys without dampening people's motivation.

3   Some senior managers apparently forget that their Core managers are people. They forget about the fears and hopes we touched on in pp. 84–8 and assume they are dealing with objective, analytical,

detached automatons. They don't really forget of course. It just looks that way from their behaviour! Instead, the Flight Crew must work with the whole person, addressing Core managers' concerns directly and taking account of any high levels of stress or emotion. To bring this about, the Flight Crew must engineer enough quality interactions to be able to understand what the Core managers value as a group, and as individuals and to reinforce the importance and high status of the new influencing role. These may be formal and planned, but unplanned and opportunistic meetings are also massively important. It is amazing how often in a day the opportunity to apply powerful positive reinforcement is declined by senior managers.

4   In order to allow people at all levels to behave as adults and to exercise appropriate degrees of initiative and responsibility in the daily performance of their roles, managers throughout the organization must establish clear Fields of Freedom (see p. 102). These must be developed in open dialogue and be explicitly stated and commonly understood. Treating people like adults is a vital part of creating strong social capital. It helps people to think for themselves, to build intellectual muscle and confidence. It allows them to feel commitment and ownership. If the Flight Crew treat their Core managers appropriately, the knock-on effect can be very positive. The converse is also true.

The following checklist is provided to help make connections between the points raised so far in this chapter and the reality in your own organization. Try them now or skip them till later as you wish. After the checklist, the chapter resumes with some thoughts on engaging Core managers, and everyone else really.

Checklist

Is this relevant to us? These questions relate to the key messages from the chapter so far. You may find them helpful in determining the extent to which a programme such as this would assist the development of healthier social capital.

In my organization:

Core managers are treated as if they make the difference between an inspiring vision and a practical reality.   I Agree/ I Disagree

All Core managers are actively engaged in developing or maintaining the level of social capital we need to excel.   I Agree/ I Disagree

We have no damp proof course or surreptitious handbrake pullers.   I Agree/ I Disagree

I don't sense any of that inexplicable drag on projects or initiatives.   I Agree/ I Disagree

There are no signs of the kinds of resistance described from Core managers. (e.g. malicious obedience, the shimmy or the dabble)   I Agree/ I Disagree

Hierarchy has either a neutral impact or makes a positive contribution to our ability to deliver successfully.   I Agree/ I Disagree

Core managers see themselves correctly as key to engaging the organization's resources in developing enhanced social capital.   I Agree/ I Disagree

Core managers know they are highly valued, both for their experience and knowledge and for their ability to engage the engine of change.   I Agree/ I Disagree

The Navigator and the Flight Crew value the Core managers highly and believe they are a major asset in engaging the organization in change.   I Agree/ I Disagree

No one at Core management level is carrying a low- or no-value label.   I Agree/ I Disagree

There is no evidence that Core managers fear failure or loss of status or control.   I Agree/ I Disagree

Core managers are happy to let go of old roles and actively embrace the new ones offered.   I Agree/ I Disagree

We have the critical mass of Core managers behind us that we need to make major change succeed.   I Agree/ I Disagree

Core managers find the rewards and recognition associated with their new role at least as attractive as the old deal.   I Agree/ I Disagree

We treat our Core managers like adults and they respond accordingly.   I Agree/ I Disagree

Both staff and Core managers are highly motivated to contribute to successful overall change through the delivery of their objectives.   I Agree/ I Disagree

Other big initiatives in the past have all delivered everything they could have.   I Agree/ I Disagree

The Flight Crew understand and employ the 'self-interest paradox' to increase the sense of belonging within the organization.   I Agree/ I Disagree

If you either answered Disagree or perhaps wished there was a 'maybe' category, then actively tackling the hearts and minds of everyone, but of the Core managers in particular, may make a significant difference to the introduction of healthier social capital in your organization as well as improving its overall performance.

Engaging Core managers in social capital

The rest of this chapter is devoted to considering what the Flight Crew must do to engage the interest and enlist the support of this most influential group to achieve the change objective. There is no easy way to do this. If it were easy then everyone would be doing it!

In order to generate low maintenance, high performance behaviour from Core managers, really engage them in developing healthy social capital and delivering excellent results, Navigator and Flight Crew must:

1   Identify and make clear what the new Core manager role entails;
2   Check that those involved understand, allowing as much input as possible on what must be tackled and how it is to be done;
3   Endow the new role with high status;
4   Make an explicit commitment to supporting behaviours;
5   Act on these commitments by (a) offering a good role model, (b) providing constant positive and negative reinforcement to embed the new behaviours, and (c) creating an environment friendly to learning and experimentation;
6   Demand an adult-to-adult relationship;
7   Negotiate and agree clear Fields of Freedom;
8   Address areas of difficulty in a sensitive but determined way, including taking hard decisions quickly and clinically where the situation demands it.

Identify and make clear the new role

Most organizations manage this part reasonably well, but still a surprising number manage to get it wrong. Those latter organizations get coy about giving out real news. They play games, even if the news is good. They fudge and equip their people with inadequate and wet woolly briefs. Naturally these are uncomfortable.

One organization we know decided to tackle chronic low morale. However, morale is a tricky subject and the brief given to the manager who was charged with rectifying things was subtle, with a lot more of the message implied than expressed. Accordingly, the manager and his project group set their sights a bit lower than they might have been or was really intended. Oh well, at least they got the restrooms repainted!

The moral of the story is that, if people do not really grasp the scope and importance of what they are being asked to do, then they will usually err on the side of caution. (See Fields of Freedom on p. 102 as a method of ensuring this does not happen.)

To avoid a rash of repainted restrooms or their organizational equivalent, managers at all levels must have the courage to be clear at the outset and to convey the true message with conviction, including any bad or difficult news.

Check that those involved understand

It is essential to ensure that the message is fully understood and not adulterated or tampered with between transmitter and recipient. The problem is that there are too many filtering agents in all but the smallest of organizations – vested interests, poor listening skills, poor transmission skills, too many messages, too many diversions, too much stress, sycophancy, fear of looking stupid – to name but a few.

The key to success is to engage in a *dialogue* not a *monologue*. Time spent helping people understand the need for, and the logic of, any new venture is well spent. A phrase from the quality management initiatives of the 1980s is still most apposite: 'I don't have time to do it right, but I do have time to do it again'. If you don't have time to get the message clear and understood at the outset, then you had better lay aside lots of time in your future plans to sort out what happens when people go away and do things you never intended.

The actual methodology of the communication process depends on the numbers. For large numbers, events based on a market stall set-up can be very cost-effective, provided the process is well positioned, structured and controlled. The Navigator may need to be present to give the signal the weight it is due. Speakeasy groups with a Flight Crew member in the hot seat are also effective, provided there is a facilitator strong enough to cope with them and the Flight Crew member is big enough to allow themselves to be robustly facilitated and challenged.

The method favoured by many is the cascade, often supported by written material. For this approach, as for any one-to-one sessions which may be necessary with key people or those who are having some difficulty with the message, it is essential to check both that the message has got through accurately and how it has been initially received.

The simple rule of thumb we have found to work again and again is for the person who has communicated the message (the transmitter) to check the understanding of the recipient(s) by asking them what they have heard – and, if that goes well, how they interpret and feel about what they have heard. This may take slightly longer than its more popular alternative, where the transmitter simply repeats the message, but it produces incomparably better results. Better too than the *transmitter* attempting to summarize, which invariably means 'putting it a different way'. Putting it a different way often results in a subtly different message to the first one – and confusion.

The return for the investment of time and effort in checking understanding can be as follows:

- The recipient has to listen.
- The recipient has to think about the message and put their own interpretation on it, because they will be using their own words when they describe to the transmitter what they believe they have heard.
- Hearing the recipient's interpretation allows any misunderstandings to be explored and cleared up at the time they are easiest to deal with – at the beginning, before inappropriate and wasteful action is taken in pursuit of the wrong goal. It is far more economical to spend the time up front.
- The process invites the recipient to engage and contribute their ideas, knowledge and experience to the way forward so that they will begin to identify with the goals of the project. In time, this will enable them to tailor the message to suit their part of the organization without adulterating and impairing its thrust.

Endow the new role with high status

Another act required of Navigator and Flight Crew is that the new role for Core managers must be given high status. The role must be introduced well and supported throughout in ways which underline its importance in delivering the future success of the organization.

Both coaching and facilitating can seem difficult and time consuming with dubious reward attached for the Core manager. The results are not always immediate or excellent. There is not always the buzz that comes from a successful rescue mission into a firefight. Influence is a bit subtler than control and the sense of achievement can be similarly thin. There may well be a sound intellectual understanding of the longer term pay-offs on the part of some Core managers, but there is also a strong human need for immediate gratification. Therefore, the subtleties of the composition of the new role must be introduced with care, sensitivity and patience and then sustained by senior managers (Flight Crew) with self-discipline and dogged determination.

Getting the Core managers started involves:

- introducing the role and giving it high status;
- getting them to challenge the role and its value add;

- getting them to truly understand and come to terms with what a typical new day would look like compared to a typical day in the past;
- providing the right kind of training environment;
- providing the right kind of support (coaching or perhaps mentoring);
- ensuring there is plenty of high profile recognition (both formal and informal).

While Coaching is a game all the Core family must play, facilitating is a more specialized function with fewer practitioners, especially at the outset. The best way forward may be to seek out people amongst the Core managers who have an aptitude for the task and a willingness to be trained. The activity can then be woven into the Key Interaction process and/or the learning sets discussed in Chapters 2 and 6 respectively. Alternatively the introduction of facilitators can be directed at project work in the initial stages. Both coaching and facilitating are discussed in greater detail in Chapter 6.

Make an explicit commitment to supporting behaviours

The key to success here lies in the personal commitment of the Flight Crew to make the transition themselves and their determination to take every opportunity to support and nurture the new behaviours in others.

In some quarters we have encountered a strong sense that major change is expected to involve everyone below a certain level in an organization and leave those above to continue much as they always have. The sentiment has been expressed quite strongly in private, and occasionally and injudiciously in public, by those who are a little too charged up in the ego department. Nothing could be further from the truth.

Acting on commitments

Offering a good role model

One of the major barriers we have found to changing individual and collective behaviour in organizations is the lack of a good role model and if that isn't part of the Flight Crew's role then one wonders what is.

That we often encounter some measure of reluctance in undertaking this responsibility is perhaps understandable. The Flight Crew are only human after all, despite the occasional allegation to the contrary. They are no more likely to relish the often uncomfortable and sometimes chastening experience of trying out new behaviours than the rest of us, and any apprehension that *does* exist can be compounded by the inevitably high profile of their role. There are, after all, plenty of people whose main purpose in organizational life seems to be to lie in wait for the boss to trip up, or 'fail to live out the values', as some might say. Glee and quiet satisfaction in some quarters! And not just that. Too many 'valuable learning experiences' by the bosses, or mistakes as most of us call them, and people may start to question how practical this vision, venture or project really is. However, despite the pitfalls, if others are required to embark on the difficult road toward social capital, it seems only reasonable for those whose idea it is, to do likewise, and, if they have to do it in the full glare of publicity, then maybe that just goes with the badge.

The key to success in this area is to manage expectations and to do so quite openly by:

- admitting to trying new things themselves because of their conviction that they will lead to a better organization;
- publicly stating that they will get it wrong and revert to type from time to time because it is difficult to change;
- enlisting the support of their people at all levels in catching them doing it right and when appropriate, wrong.

In this way, the shared journey effect is brought in to replace that laboratory animal feeling, which is common when the only people required to change is us. The argument goes like this. 'If coaching is such a good thing, it would be nice to see the boss doing it. If it is difficult to change to an influencing role from a controlling one, then it would be nice to see the boss dropping off his perch from time to time – even nicer if we could bring it to his/her attention without drastically affecting our career prospects.'

This applies to all the behaviours, attitudes and skills required of Core managers and others in order to develop social capital. Those above in the hierarchy should not ask others to do what they are not prepared to do themselves. Not a new thought admittedly, but a practice which is more often omitted than observed. One final note of warning. If the invitation to 'catch me when I revert to type' is to be accepted, then Navigator and Flight Crew must not be defensive when challenged. A few defensive responses and the word will go round that the boss is not serious. There will be no more challenges and a major engine of change will be gone.

This highlights the very real difficulties of bridging the gap between good intentions and good behaviour, between intellectual understanding about what is right and carrying it into practice in a live working environment. And, as if that weren't enough, there is one further obligation on those who would be positive role models. Once you start you must not stop!

An example of this that we experienced, occurred when 'Management by Walking About' first arrived on the scene. At one of their meetings, the MD and Board of a company agreed that MBWA was a very good thing and that it could pay significant dividends in performance and morale.

Recognizing the need for a blunt instrument, they all agreed that every Tuesday they would MBWA. Then someone pointed out that next Tuesday wasn't good because the Group President was visiting. Then another chipped in that, come to think of it, the following Tuesday was no good either because ... Need we go on? The obvious conclusion you might draw is that MBWA never happened. Not so! The truth is worse than that. It happened for a little while with some directors – just enough to raise expectations, but not of course enough to fulfil them. 'Just another passing fad', the old sweats remarked as they got stuck into a ticklish operational problem that they had solved at least three times in one shape or another over the last ten years. Once you start you must persevere.

Providing constant positive and negative reinforcement for the new behaviours

Their new role will take up a lot of the Core manager's time, particularly in the early stages. It will require some faith and determination to stay with it. The Flight Crew must provide at least some of this through persistent and sustained reinforcement, both positive and negative. However, even more is required of them. There are certain of their *own* behaviours which must also change and here we are not talking about being a role model, as earlier.

People involved in change which is not their own idea, are usually very alert for signals that it is OK to revert to the old ways. Naturally they will look to their bosses for a lead in this. The Flight Crew must take great pains not to give out such signals. So where previously they would ask about tasks, problems and projects, the topic of conversation now must be more about strategy, people and performance. This will demand considerable self-discipline and vigilance because it is all too easy to inadvertently give out the wrong message. To do so, all that is required is to ask operational questions of the Core manager with the apparent expectation that they will have the information at their fingertips.

The problem is that the 'reconstructed' Core manager is not doing that any more. If they are really concentrating on coaching, their knowledge will be second hand at best. When they are forced to admit ignorance on the subject, they feel bad. They wonder what the Flight Crew member really thinks of them now. They don't want to take the chance of being viewed in a bad light, particularly with so many changes going on. They take steps to make sure it doesn't happen again, and right there, the rot will begin to set in. The Core manager will have a quiet word with their staff and agree it would be best to provide a brief report each morning just to ensure that 'everyone' is kept fully abreast of what is going on. Thus, further embarrassment is saved and we are well on the road back to the old role. The Core manager feels happier and more comfortable. Of course they do. They can now spend a few minutes first thing each morning listening to, or reading, reports on operational issues. 'And it is just as well!' they tell themselves, because they find things that are not going quite as they would make them go or they see things they could help with. That must surely still be a part of their job! So they intervene. Ah, they sigh, as they settle back into the comfortable armchair of their old role. Now that feels better!

The message to the troops is now at best mixed. The ones who have thrown themselves into the new ways feel disappointed and lost. People who have stuck their necks out for the new cause feel betrayed (or worse, embarrassed) and vow never to do so again. The shaggy-lock shakers who 'always knew this was just another fad' smile knowingly and are vindicated as they go about in the old fashioned way. All is well and nothing is changing and all because the Flight Crew asked one question out of place. Fantasy? No. Perhaps a little dramatization for effect, but this or something like it happens regularly.

The key message is that people are very sensitive to what they think the boss thinks is important, so every act and every reference must be positioned in terms of the delivery of the desired change. This means:

- that whenever a member of the Flight Crew is planning a task with a Core manager, discussing its progress, or reviewing its outcome, they should always make a point of asking how this will help deliver better social capital.
- that when personal and unit goals are set for the year, they must include the delivery of social capital. It is surprising how often this one is missed and such an omission can readily be seized upon as a signal.
- recognizing success (as well as unfulfilled effort) informally at every opportunity.
- creating formal ways of recognizing progress such as appearances at senior management meetings.
- exercising self-restraint when they want to know about some operational details and reminding themselves who is now likely to have such information.

Creating an environment friendly to learning and experimentation

It is important to address and reduce any anxiety about newness by helping Core managers get familiar with the demands and behaviours implicit in the new role in a low-profile, non-threatening environment.

Core managers are being asked to make a difficult transition from expert controller to adept facilitator and coach. They are being asked to master these new and uncomfortable skills, while at the same time keeping the whole operation running. They must not be rewarded for their courage and their energy by allowing their people to get ahead of them. It is not intended that they should be masters of everything their people do, but rather that they should have enough of any new technology or terminology or behavioural approach to keep face in any dialogue.

The key message is that Core managers should be kept ahead of the game so that they can feel good about themselves and their new role and can engage wholeheartedly without fear of exposure.

Let them learn the new ways slowly if that is what is required. Use a learning styles preference questionnaire (Honey and Mumford) to help them identify the way they like to learn best and give them the space, the support and the encouragement to get on with it.

Demand an adult-to-adult relationship

Another behaviour required of the Navigator and Flight Crew is to treat people with respect – as adults not children. It is worth finding a good text on Transactional Analysis, if you think this may be an issue.

In essence, the aim in developing social capital must be to create and maintain adult-to-adult relationships throughout the organization. That is to say, the relationships should be based on shared responsibility. They must therefore be authentic, honest and respectful, whilst also being challenging and confronting.

Often in change, the relationship is parent to child. Who the instigator may be, Flight Crew or those below, is largely immaterial. Once the dance has begun, the relationship is self-reinforcing and can only be broken by determined effort and courage. One version of the dance, for example, is that Core managers become aware that they are being treated in a non-adult way. They can either protest or take more covert action. Most take the latter. They may choose to deliver the behaviours that their treatment invites – the self-fulfilling prophecy we discussed on p. 87 or invent some other equally dreadful response. On the other hand, where the instigator of the parent/child relationship is the Core manager, they may reject all overtures on the part of 'the leadership', behaving instead rather like a huffy and recalcitrant child in spite of all attempts to treat them with respect. In these circumstances the Flight Crew must show great restraint and forego the temptation to act like a parent.

Fear and anxiety lie at the heart of much of the opposition offered. These causes are often overlooked or dismissed by Flight Crew who can sometimes appear to get hooked on a kind of 'big managers don't cry' philosophy; also perhaps because they can be time consuming to tackle and still fail due to other factors. However, if the alternative is to lose a valuable resource completely, or retain a potential saboteur, the return on the investment from actively addressing these issues can be very worthwhile. When doing so, in order to avoid a self-indulgent wallow, the emphasis on adult/adult behaviour must be maintained throughout, so as to keep the responsibility for finding a productive way forward a joint one. Thus, the offer is made to engage the whole person. Approaches include listening and providing emotional support, recognizing stress by giving people time off after a demanding period and even trusting Core managers with all the facts and asking them to engage to find a solution. This last option is one of the principles of the Field of Freedom described in the next section.

The pay-off is that the workforce will have real evidence that their well-being is seen as important. People will feel valued and when it becomes apparent that they are expected to contribute to finding a solution, they feel trusted as well. At the same time they realize that this is not an easy ride. With adulthood comes responsibility.

Negotiate and agree clear Fields of Freedom

One way to equip people to behave like adults is to negotiate clear Fields of Freedom. These define what constraints are present in relation to each person's role and hence the amount of scope they have to exercise freedom, judgement, initiative and creativity within those constraints. It is particularly important where there is a need to free up a Core manager so that they can bring their skills, knowledge and experience to bear and feel a real sense of contribution to the delivery of goals.

Other uses include goal setting, delegation, coaching and supporting, establishing the scope of a project or the individual roles within it; any dialogue which requires a common and clear understanding about roles and goals in fact.

The process is based on the concept that if the boundaries are unclear, most people do not try to take on the world or bet the firm. Instead they will err on the side of caution, be less adventurous, less creative, contribute less of themselves and achieve less. The boundary areas they abandon become no-man's-land; grey areas of inactivity, which get lost and ignored until they emerge from the fog as problems and often expensive afterthoughts, requiring urgent Flight Crew attention. Curiously, the imposition of con-straints or boundaries on the scope of a role, when these are fully discussed, understood and accepted, act to free up the performer of the role, because everything within the Field boundaries is theirs. Once agreed, no one, including their manager has the right to step onto that Field without checking first. Scary for both parties to deal with at first of course, not least because many managers implicitly reserve the right to nip onto the field and kick the metaphorical ball a bit when their team isn't doing too well; thereby not only justifying their existence but bringing that feel-good rush of being a rescuer as well. Does the self-esteem no end of good! Unfortunately it doesn't help their people grow into full-scale contributors, so in social capital terms it is not acceptable.

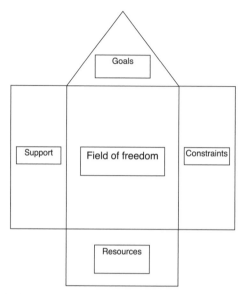

Figure 4.1. Field of Freedom.

The Field of Freedom is a simple but powerful multi-purpose tool which produces significant benefits for a remarkably small investment. It provides a graphic map to help you navigate through the process and subsequently check that nothing of importance has been left out (Figure 4.1 shows what is looks like).

When working with the Field of Freedom, it is vital to be very clear about the goals involved and to check that these are fully understood. Any constraints must also be discussed and accepted. The support required from the manager, the form it will take and when it will happen should also be explicit. The resources area should be discussed in detail. Sending someone off to do a job without the wherewithall is a recipe for failure. Resources in this context refer to anything that will help get the task done efficiently and successfully – time, training, money, equipment, people, skills, information – the list goes on. The Field itself and the real meaning of the freedom on offer must also be clear to both parties. All agreement must be genuine and specific. It takes a bit of time, but this process really engages people.

Address areas of difficulty and recognize when action is required

Barriers to progress

As you may now know we have been occasionally surprised to encounter a view which seems to imply that, as mature adults drawing a reasonable pay,

Core managers are unlikely to have much in the way of feelings and emotions. Bizarre of course, but quite enlightening in terms of the way they are sometimes handled during major change. In fact, while a few of the barriers which people erect in the face of change, may be based on a logical and objective assessment of the pros and cons of a particular change, the majority seem to have their roots in more subjective soil.

The thoughts offered below have been selected for their harmony with the development of social capital. Although applicable to people throughout the organization, we have kept the focus here on Core managers.

Some of the more 'popular' barriers are:

- a feeling that what is being proposed is not right;
- an assessment by the Core manager that it is not in their interest;
- a worry that they may lose prestige or standing in the community;
- being faced with losing a part of their lives that they have enjoyed, a particular piece of work or the opportunity to work with a specific person or group, for instance;
- a concern that they may lose out, relative to certain colleagues;
- a perceived or actual reduction in power or hierarchical status;
- a general feeling of unease surrounding this latest uncertainty about the future;
- even something akin to bereavement at the loss of what they consider to be the deal they had with the 'old' organization;
- the loss of a job for life;
- loss or lack of trust;
- a deep sense of weariness, a change too far, initiative fatigue. When people feel they have had enough, they find ways to call a halt to the experience;
- concerns about the potential for failure, loss of face and embarrassment;
- perceived or actual loss of control.

Just to elaborate on one of these, trust; even if Core managers hear the message that the new coaching and facilitating role is going to be as high if not higher status than the old control-oriented one, will they choose to believe it? There are likely to be two elements which may colour their judgement in this matter; sincerity and credibility. People must have confidence that those above them know what they are doing and will do what they are saying they will do. Trust is based on the consistency between words and deeds in the past. Unlike faith, trust must be earned. The good news is that this makes it possible to start even from a basis of mistrust and work towards a more trusting relationship in a series of small steps. It makes it a long road of course, so best not to start there if you can avoid it.

Tackling the barriers

When change is taking place, the amount of quality communication should increase dramatically. What happens in most cases is that true quality communication dwindles to almost nothing. Oh there is a lot of information floating around, but it isn't structured and focused and it isn't attributable – it isn't quality. When there is an information vacuum, people get anxious and fill it with concoctions of their own making which are most unlikely to coincide with the views of those initiating the particular change. Rumour and the grapevine dominate. These are rarely positive and the negative atmosphere which is generated gives rise to precautionary and defence-building activity. In the absence of any credible guidance to the contrary, Core managers begin to build their survival strategies around these various interpretations of reality. Political behaviours become more common. As a result, initiators of change, suddenly sallying forth with their ideas already well formed and expecting a reasonably positive if not rapturous reception, can be dismayed, mystified and hurt by the negative reception they receive – often even when the news is good.

The only way to prevent this is by increasing the amount of quality two-way communication, and just at the time when there is so much else to do too. The cost of not doing so is great, however. When people are anxious and in the dark, any willingness to subordinate self-interest to the greater good is likely to diminish.

The form the communication strategy takes must obviously depend on the circumstances of the organization in question. Size, geographical and functional dispersion, the type of workforce and recent history must all play a part, to name but a few. However, in addition to the exhortation to communicate like mad, there are a few principles which hold good across the board and which are consistent with the development of healthier social capital.

First, it is essential to try to avoid the non-productive strategies, the ones that might work in the short term but which would effectively destroy the prospects of developing the inclusive atmosphere so necessary for a sense of community to come about. These include making people feel guilty for not co-operating, threatening them, giving them a hard sell with all the razzamatazz, ridiculing any fears that are expressed, or simply ignoring any negative vibes in the hope that they will go away. Tempting, perhaps, but definitely not on the social capital agenda.

Second, it is essential to engage in a *dialogue*, not a monologue, and that dialogue had better be about what the Core managers want to talk about. It sounds as though this could be time consuming and indeed it might just be, often because the full story does not emerge at the first attempt. Sometimes this is because trust is not there, sometimes because of embarrassment and it can even be that the Core manager isn't all that sure why they feel the way they do. Whatever the reason, the dialogue must move along at its own pace and must be conducted by the Flight Crew with infinite patience and skill. Whether it is a good investment of time must be a judgement call which takes into account all the prevailing conditions. Unfortunately however, sometimes the only way to really make progress and still have the people behind you and not behind the barriers, is to show you value the whole person, fears, emotions, hang-ups and all. This may sound a bit soft and peoply but in fact can feel very confronting for all parties concerned.

When you start to feel the pressure of events elsewhere and begin to question the wisdom of having embarked on this course, cling to your conviction that the ultimate goal is worth having, and that, without this investment of time, all the energy which could have been redirected towards the creation of a great place to work will be squandered on negative strategies. In the event that co-operation is not forthcoming from a few in the timescale required, we suggest that the hard decisions are taken quickly, clearly and without sentimentality. In the long run, the majority will understand and respect that approach more than the dreadful, long-drawn-out, sawing and hacking that frequently goes on in the name of kindness. Sometimes the scalpel must by wielded to preserve the whole. If this is required, it should be done swiftly and with conviction and surety.

Back to the subject of meaningful dialogues. These may take place one to one or between a Flight Crew and a small group. The plusses and minuses of each are fairly obvious, but the steps are the same. We see four that will apply generally; namely, analysing and preparing for the encounter, making sure the rules of the game are understood at the outset, ensuring that the root cause of any negativity is really identified, and, producing a jointly agreed way forward for the future. Because of the particular focus of this chapter on Core managers, we have used a Flight Crew/Core manager dialogue as an example, but these steps are universal.

Step 1

The Flight Crew member should spend some time thinking about the Core manager, their character, their ways of behaving and any historical baggage they may bring with them. Give some thought also to how the Core manager(s) are likely to be viewing the proposed changes. This process of tuning in to others' feelings and perspectives on the issue will pay dividends when the time comes, in first understanding and then jointly confronting the barriers to progress with authenticity and realism. Lastly, check out your own feelings on the subject and the individual. Are they likely to be helpful in solving the problem?

Step 2

At the start of the meeting, it is important to be clear about the purpose and the way the meeting is to be conducted. If there have been specific instances of negative behaviour, be sure to describe them and not to label the Core manager instead. State clearly your positive intent for the outcome and the future working relationship. Be prepared to make these statements as many times during the meeting as necessary. Ask for their help in making the meeting a success and as the meeting progresses, keep on asking. Be patient in the face of denials or defensive noises and make sure the other person understands that this conversation *will* take place and that it is important.

Step 3

This is the meat of the process. There is no guarantee of a breakthrough, but they do come, and sometimes they come surprisingly quickly. On the other hand, this step may take more than one meeting. There are often other dynamics at work which prolong the process. The Flight Crew may find themselves under attack and the focus of accusations of blame. They would only be human if they felt inclined to defend, or explain or hit back, yet they must not. Explanations may make the Flight Crew feel better, but they let the Core manager off the hook. Instead, a coaching approach should be adopted. This provides a strong indication to the Core manager that they are required to take some responsibility for finding a solution and that their help is essential if that solution is to prove a good fit with the real problem. Without their active co-operation, it must be made clear, the outcome is much less likely to be a happy one. They may feel like a hurt child, and that is OK for a while, but ultimately they must act like a responsible adult. By the end of step 3, it is necessary to have jointly got to the root cause.

Step 4

By this stage the hard work has been done and it is all too easy to sit back with a self-congratulatory sigh and take your eye off the ball. Instead, it is essential to build on the good work and be very specific about what is going to happen next and who is going to do what, when and how. The Field of Freedom can be used, if you like. To be able to do this, there has to be a common understanding of what has changed as a result of steps 1–3, so some checking of understanding would be useful. This should cover both facts and feelings.

Throughout the whole process, certain skills and behaviours are key. The ability to listen well and to use techniques like reflecting, to ask questions which help and avoid those which don't, to really probe for specificity, to show a willingness to deal with feelings and emotions, to maintain a determined refusal to be fobbed off with red herrings and an insistence that the outcome is a joint responsibility – all these must be employed. The Flight Crew member must choose and use behaviours which foster an adult-to-adult relationship. If they allow the Core manager to cast them in the role of the nasty parent then the Core manager is off the hook yet again.

In fact the Flight Crew member must be very disciplined in their whole performance, not least because a lot of these are skills used in coaching and as such there is a high degree of role modelling on view for the Core manager. They must be able to state clearly and specifically what the purpose of the meeting is and not lose sight of that in the twists and turns of discussion. If necessary they must remember to give frequent reminders if it looks as though the session is turning into a self-indulgent wallow. This is not therapy. It is a conversation with a purpose. On the other hand, the Flight Crew must not rush to judgement or be dismissive of emotions or perceptions which may be deeply felt or firmly held. Lastly they must never forget that the final grand objective is an organization rich in healthy social capital and delivering consistently excellent performance.

A final note

In this chapter we have focused on winning over the hearts and minds of the Core managers but the styles and processes are applicable to all those involved in the development of healthy social capital. If all this seems too much, it is worth bearing in mind: 'I don't have time to do it right, but I do have time to do it again – and again – and again – and again'.

Specific ways of working at present

Engaging Core managers is essential for effecting a major step change in performance and then holding onto it. These questions may help you determine what specific ways of working, which currently prevail within your organization, should change in order to make the most of the positive power waiting to be tapped in the ranks of your Core managers.

In my organization:

The Flight Crew show explicitly every day that they value Core managers for their knowledge and experience.　I Agree/I Disagree

The Flight Crew take the time to ensure that Core managers know that knowledge and experience are only part of the contribution they are required to make.　I Agree/I Disagree

The Flight Crew make the time to ensure that Core managers know what else they must contribute – exactly!　I Agree/I Disagree

Core managers are typically engaged in low maintenance, high-performance interactions.　I Agree/I Disagree

Core managers act like they believe that influence gives them more status than control.　I Agree/I Disagree

Core managers will tell anyone who will listen about their new high-status role as coach and facilitator.	I Agree/I Disagree
Core managers can tell you in detail the last time in the last few days they were given some positive reinforcement about their influencing role by their immediate boss.	I Agree/I Disagree
Core managers act in ways which suggest they enjoy their new roles and find them just as rewarding as the old ones.	I Agree/I Disagree
Core managers have explicit Fields of Freedom developed and agreed in dialogue with their boss.	
Core managers understand their Fields of Freedom and can give practical examples of these in application.	I Agree/I Disagree
Core managers have established clear Fields of Freedom with their staff.	I Agree/I Disagree
If you asked staff what their Field of Freedom was in detail, their explanation would coincide exactly with the one you would get from their manager.	I Agree/I Disagree
Core managers use their powerful position to constantly remind staff of the behaviours which develop healthier social capital.	I Agree/I Disagree
Core managers assist their staff every day to cross functional boundaries in the pursuit of success.	I Agree/I Disagree
Core managers spend a major part of their working day in coaching and supporting their staff.	I Agree/I Disagree
Both Navigator and Flight Crew take active steps to identify and address individual and collective concerns surrounding major change.	I Agree/I Disagree
There is no evidence of the shimmy or the dabble or any other of these negative behaviours.	I Agree/I Disagree
The Flight Crew can be observed on a daily basis working to identify and meet both the self-interest of Core managers and their need to belong.	I Agree/I Disagree
The Flight Crew are active in creating many high quality interactions with all Core managers.	I Agree/I Disagree
Navigator and Flight Crew make opportunities on a daily basis to reinforce the importance and high status of the new influencing role.	I Agree/I Disagree
Formal opportunities to enhance the status of the role are arranged frequently.	I Agree/I Disagree

If you either answered Disagree or perhaps wished there was a 'maybe' category, then actively tackling ways of working could make a major difference to the introduction of healthier social capital in your organization as well as improve its overall performance.

Skills, behaviours and attitudes

These questions may help you assess the extent to which the Core managers in your organization already exhibit the essential behaviours, skills and attitudes necessary to support the introduction of social capital effectively.

In my organization, Core managers:

Are fully committed to the achievement of social capital.   I Agree/I Disagree

Are skilled coaches. They ask questions in ways that help.   I Agree/I Disagree

Are skilled facilitators. They know and can apply a range of   I Agree/I Disagree
facilitative tools competently.

Are excellent listeners and use this skill to enhance relationships   I Agree/I Disagree
and so to improve performance.

Show good skill in negotiating Fields of Freedom with their boss.   I Agree/I Disagree

Show good skill in negotiating Fields of Freedom with their staff.   I Agree/I Disagree

Treat their staff as responsible and committed adults.   I Agree/I Disagree

Are skilled in a range of leadership styles.   I Agree/I Disagree

Are skilled in selecting the best style appropriate to the specific   I Agree/I Disagree
circumstances.

Are skilled at confronting conflict (between goals, between   I Agree/I Disagree
perceptions, between individuals and between groups) so that
enhanced working relationships occur and performance is
enhanced.

Are good at identifying what motivates different individuals and   I Agree/I Disagree
skilled at finding ways to engage them.

Are skilled at addressing failure or poor performance in others   I Agree/I Disagree
in ways that enhance relationships and improve future
performance.

Show they are in tune by regularly making good strategic decisions   I Agree/I Disagree
within their Fields of Freedom.

If you either answered Disagree or perhaps wished there was a 'maybe' category, then some behavioural training may make a significant difference to the introduction of healthier social capital in your organization as well as improving its overall performance.

Chapter 5

Delivering the goods

While it is true that without a vision the people perish, it is doubly true
that without action, both the people and the vision perish

J. B. COLE

In organizational terms, a vision without the means to turn it into reality
might as well be a hallucination. If it is the Navigator who creates the vision
that inspires, the Flight Crew who create the strategic momentum and the
Core managers whose task it is to engage all the necessary resources, then it
is the Activators who turn it into practical form.

By our definition, the Activators are the first-line managers and some
of their key people – opinion formers, who are not necessarily managers but
who occupy particularly influential roles for example – also certain technical
people and specialists who are paid at higher rates because of labour market
forces. They are the people who make things happen on a day-to-day basis
at operational level and in the final analysis, deliver the goods. They make
the ideas work. They build on them. They are a source of practical wisdom.
When they are engaged and feel a real sense of belonging, they effect the
minor adjustments to ideas, systems and processes that are always needed to
bridge the gap between theory and practice. The term Activator is therefore
defined more by function than hierarchical position.

In this chapter we examine how these people can be fully engaged in
delivering healthier social capital along with business success and offer a
means of achieving this through an integrated modular training and development programme which uses momentum and relevance to achieve a
critical mass of new ways of working.

Activators have the potential to make a number of telling contributions to the development and subsequent maintenance of healthy social
capital. For example, they often represent a significant source of future
leaders and managers. Amongst their ranks are graduate entrants fresh

from university and business school, young less academically inclined talent promoted from the shop floor, and late maturers with their wealth of practical experience and knowledge. For all these very different people, even those who by choice or circumstance progress no further up the organizational hierarchy, the experience of being an Activator will stay with them, conditioning their views and actions and ways of working for the rest of their organizational lives. So as an investment for the future, making that formative experience a positive one for Activators, is likely to be second to none.

There are many ways of investing in healthier social capital and fostering a greater sense of belonging, shared journey and commitment to the common cause, to replace the factional contests which so often dominate the interactions at this level. We touch on some of these in the final chapter and there are now many articles and quite a few new books which do justice to these ways. However, as you know, our preoccupation in this book is with behaviours and processes and ways of working. Initiatives in these areas, like for instance the Total Quality Management (TQM) phenomenon of the 1980s, tend to be introduced as a number of big ideas supported by prescribed processes and heavy investment in training and development. In this chapter we are concerned with training and developing the Activators, and in particular, how to create a critical mass of people all of whom are going through a similar learning and growing experience at the same time. Never an easy task when people are also required to keep the organization functioning, but one which can and has been done with very impressive results.

The keys to success in this area are coherence, momentum and relevance, just the places that traditional training and development programmes often fall short. Where such training is piecemeal and uncoordinated this is understandable but even where there has been a considerable investment in an organization-wide suite of training and development products, excellent workshop design and high quality tutors, results tend to fall disappointingly short of expectations. The main problem, even with products of excellent quality, is that they fail to engage the right people and not just that, they fail to engage enough of the right people at one time. Core managers, for example, can easily be seduced into viewing a list of centrally sponsored training and development courses as a kind of candy store from which they can select the tastiest morsels for their deserving, and indeed their undeserving people. That they do not feel personally involved in these circumstances is witnessed by the frequent lack of pre-workshop positioning given to participants and the absence of much in the way of post-workshop debriefing and subsequent work-related action. The fact is that many Core managers are invited by such a process to see training and development as something which exists at arm's length from their central business. Such a view will not deliver healthy social capital. Instead, to develop the necessary sense of belonging and shared journey, they must be actively engaged to the extent that they are an integral part of the whole experience.

Another problem with traditional training and development is that the effect is too dissipated. With numbers of Core managers from different functions bidding for places on a range of workshops pre-scheduled for the forthcoming months and sometimes years, the chances of more than a very few Activators from any one unit going through the same experience at the same time are very slim. The result is that the impact on ways of working is far less than the quality of the immediate workshop experience might deserve. Instead what is required is an intense, powerful experience which is shared by all the Activators within a certain operational radius over a short period of time. This produces not only the desired critical mass which is a tremendous help in changing collective behaviour, but also a strong sense of energy and momentum and a high degree of peer support for those who need it – which at some time or another is virtually all of us.

And lastly there is the question of relevance. It is vital that Activators see training and development as relevant to them and the work they do. In reality, a lot of the time they know that all they need do in order to weather the storm of new initiatives, training and development among them, is to *appear* to go along, whilst at the same time conducting their business much as they always did. They have learned from experience that these are often transient gusts of wind, which do little more than temporarily ruffle the feathers of the bird corporate, or for that matter, the individual of the species. Naturally, however pragmatic such a philosophy may be, it is anathema to leaders and drivers of change. They want and need engagement. They want commitment, not lip service. They want to know that the hearts and minds, so essential for developing healthy social capital, have been won. They want a workforce which personally identifies with the objectives of the organization, and which is prepared to give more of itself in exchange for the privilege of belonging.

To bring this about and also to maximize its positive impact on performance, any training and development must be given explicit relevance to the Activators' workplace reality. It must have meaning for them. It must strike a chord. It must address issues they care about and help make their lives more satisfying or successful or whatever lights their particular fire. Most of all, if it is to become an important part of their way of life, it must have immediate applicability. To achieve this, any programme design must place great emphasis on applying learning immediately to *real* work tasks.

Our argument so far has suggested that, in order to develop healthier social capital at Activator level, any initiative must have relevance, coherence and momentum. There is one more thing however. If, as we propose in Chapter 4, it is essential to the development of healthy social capital that Core managers relinquish much of their day-to-day control over events and instead become coaches, facilitators, strategic thinkers and planners, then it follows that there must be a similarly radical change in the way the Activators go about *their* daily business. They must become less dependent on their bosses as sources of ready advice, knowledge and experience, and find other ways to access these vital ingredients of success. Therefore any programme aimed at generating a sense of common purpose across the whole organization must offer a means of facilitating such a state of affairs. It must create the conditions for networks to spring up spontaneously and to feel so natural that people don't even use the word. They simply think of it as the way we do things around here now. They just do it, crossing functional boundaries as if they weren't there, which of course they really aren't!

The Activators are the seedcorn of the organization. Regardless of the differences in individual destinies, their behaviour holds the key not just to an organization's present performance, but also to its future social capital. Creating the right conditions for Activators now, therefore offers a double return on investment. They will not only begin to perform more effectively and efficiently in the short term. They will also pass the new ways on to others and soon these will become accepted as the norm. The aim is, in a reasonably short space of time, to create a working environment that is robust, self-sustaining and self-improving.

A way forward – or not

There is no hiding the fact that the programme we suggest is a most demanding one. However it is also tried and tested. In 1997 it won a National (UK) Training Award which was presented jointly to our company, TW Associates, and one of our clients, a Division of United Distillers, now UDV. It has also been applied successfully elsewhere.

For those who would like a bit of background colour, here is a brief overview of the UDV programme. If you are not familiar with the company, they are a major drinks manufacturer, now part of Diageo. World famous products include Guinness, Gordons and Tanqueray Gin, wines and of course whisky. The division in question was responsible for looking after the company's whisky production from the time it was manufactured till it was due to be blended and bottled as Johnnie Walker, Bells, Dimple, White Horse and so on.

Including all the preparatory work, the programme ran from September 1994 to December 1996. There were forty-three Activator participants drawn from several sites across Scotland, all of whom found themselves in new and more demanding roles as a result of a recent reorganization which had flattened the structure of their division considerably. Just about every possible variation of age, ambition, ability, background and motivation was represented. The functions they were responsible for were equally varied.

The programme we ran on this occasion had all the elements described later in the chapter. There were 14 modules plus the essential familiarization and Core managers' prep sessions. Due to the numbers involved, we ran it in three tranches of approximately fifteen participants per workshop. To create momentum and a critical mass of new behaviours, the three workshops were always run back to back. In this case, the modules included subjects like working with pressure, negotiating, working assertively, creating a motivated workforce, managing resources and looking after your customers. There is a fuller list of possible subjects on p. 129.

The formal post-programme evaluation and assessment for the award concluded that the programme had been 'highly successful' and identified the following as some of the pay-offs.

- Top managers were now much more relaxed about delegating and this had 'released them to undertake a wider remit including forward planning' and involve themselves in 'more strategically important issues.'
- Each Core manager was able to run more sites than before, producing a saving estimated at more than £100,000 per year.
- Participants at Activator level had taken on much more of the day-to-day running of the sites and were perceived by their people as being more willing to share information, decision making and problem solving. There was now a strong feeling of 'belonging to one unit' and a dramatic 'increase in network contacts across the Division' where barriers and boundaries had existed in the past. Also identified was a 'noticeable willingness to implement change faster, to take a positive attitude towards and to manage change more effectively.'
- A number of the Activators themselves were seen as having been transformed by the process. One typical comment was, 'We now share ideas, success and failures. We learn from each other instead of trying to reinvent the wheel on our own each time.' Another noticed that 'The level of trust between us has increased. We look, feel and operate much more like a team.'
- Productivity in one of the key measurements had risen by 30.2% over the two years, and 'the pooling of skill, knowledge and experience across sites' had resulted in 'substantial savings' over the same period including a reduction in overtime costs of £500,000.
- Staff numbers had reduced by 2% and the number of Activators required to deliver the goods for the Division had shrunk to 35 as a result of the efficiencies produced by the programme. These two factors alone had produced an additional saving of £300,000 per annum.

As the one-off, direct costs of running the programme were only a fraction of the savings, which were themselves on-going, the return on investment can be regarded as quite respectable. In terms of healthier social capital they were considerable and a credit to the organization.

After the checklist which follows this paragraph, we describe how the programme can be run, but before we do, it is essential to sound a note of caution. Despite all the positive vibes above, it is important to recognize that this programme design is not as easy as other training because it places demands on everyone – their time and commitment and their own ways of working. It is not candy store training with its arm's-length relationship between the training and the managers who recommend it for their people. It should only be embarked upon if there is a real need, coupled with a determination to change things. The managers at UDV had that, and it sustained them through the difficult times and brought them success. If the Flight Crew and the Core are not committed, don't even think about this programme.

Checklist

This checklist focuses on the issues raised in the chapter so far and is offered as an aid to assessing their relevance to your organization. Try it now or skip it till later as you wish.

In my organization:

Activators already make a full and positive contribution to the development of healthier social capital.	I Agree/I Disagree
Training and development (T&D) activities have coherence, momentum and relevance.	I Agree/I Disagree
T&D delivers all we can expect of it.	I Agree/I Disagree
We do not indulge in candy store T&D.	I Agree/I Disagree
Pre- and post-workshop positioning is excellent.	I Agree/I Disagree
Core managers see developing Activators as a key part of their role.	I Agree/I Disagree
T&D activities are concentrated for maximum impact.	I Agree/I Disagree
T&D activities employ a high degree of peer support to achieve tangible results.	I Agree/I Disagree

T&D activities have real meaning for the Activators and address issues they care about.	I Agree/I Disagree
Activators personally identify with the objectives of the organization.	I Agree/I Disagree
T&D activities have immediate application to real work tasks.	I Agree/I Disagree
T&D activities encourage Activators to work as if functional boundaries did not exist.	I Agree/I Disagree
The effects of T&D can be seen spreading out from those immediately involved.	I Agree/I Disagree
The Flight Crew are visibly committed to achieving performance improvement through T&D.	I Agree/I Disagree
We treat our Activator population as the seedcorn of the future.	I Agree/I Disagree
T&D programmes create the critical mass necessary to effect collective behaviour change.	I Agree/I Disagree
T&D activities in the past have always represented an excellent return on investment.	I Agree/I Disagree

If you either answered Disagree or perhaps wished there was a 'maybe' category, then a programme of the type we describe for the Activators may make a significant difference to the introduction of healthier social capital in your organization, as well as improving its overall performance.

The principal features of the programme

In this section we look at the modular nature of the programme, the support required to achieve maximum impact and the pay-offs and pitfalls associated with a design such as this.

The modules

Each module period typically lasts between 6 and 8 weeks and is devoted to one subject. The title 'module' therefore can be seen to encompass not just workshops but *all* activities by *all* active players. As each module ends, the next one begins without a break. It feels inexorable and so it should, but it is also exciting and energizing. Modules can focus in on any subject which is seen as a priority in its likely impact on the organization's ability to perform and to develop its social capital. This process of selecting module subjects for maximum impact in the current stage of an organization's development is described in the third section of this chapter, under the heading of Steering Group. The need to select subjects which build on one another is also important, as it provides a sense of purpose and a meaning to the journey. This is considered further in the paragraphs on Shape and Flow (see pp. 127–8).

Modular programmes are effective because most behaviour change takes place incrementally in small, frequent steps. Workshops are of short duration to reflect this. In addition, a soundly based, actively supported modular programme creates a sense of progress, of excitement and involvement. It feels like a shared journey and it feels to people like they are really getting somewhere. When enough people move far enough along the path of incremental behavioural change, a critical mass is achieved and the new ways become the norm.

Workshops and applying the learning

In a very real sense workshops are the least important of the module activities. Their role is simply to provide the initial experience of new behaviours and processes in a relatively safe environment. With this design they are *not* the place to master the new ways. That is best done in the real work environment, focused on real work tasks and with the support of appropriate colleagues. In this way learning can be applied immediately on return and applied not as a fanciful addition to the daily workload but as an aid to the achievement of regular work objectives. This lends weight and meaning to the new ways, which is essential if they are to be seen as worthy of the investment of finite time and energy.

Support

This is required in two forms – personal support which is responsive to changing organization priorities as well as to individual and collective development needs, and system support which is tough and inflexible enough to withstand the pressures of other urgent demands on time, resources and attention. It is the curious combination of high responsiveness and inflexibility which gives the design part its unusual feel.

Personal support comes from a number of sources. Core managers, acting as coaches, must focus Activators on practical applications for their learning as soon as they return from the workshops. Without their active involvement, even the best training and development suffers from burn up, on re-entry to the workplace. Where behaviours are concerned, learning which is not applied immediately is usually learning lost. Plans to apply the learning must not be seen as some kind of barely affordable luxury, inconvenient diversion or manufactured add-on to the real work. Core managers can help greatly by identifying areas where real operational value-add can be obtained. They are also vital in helping overcome any opposition to the new ways of working which may be encountered in the shape of status issues, entrenched positions and old enmities.

The Flight Crew have two major roles to play in supporting the application of new learning. The first involves their interaction with the Core managers, who must be encouraged to see the drive to develop the Activators as a worthwhile investment of their time and energies. The Flight Crew must convince them that such an investment is both in their own interests and personally status enhancing. The importance of winning the hearts and minds of this key group cannot be overstated. The power they possess to influence practical events on the ground is second to none. They have the necessary gravitas and street cred to make things happen, and the opportunity to exert major influence accorded by proximity and frequent contact with the Activator population. Without their active involvement and commitment the programme will just not happen in any meaningful way. The responsibility for bringing this about lies with the Flight Crew.

The second vital role for the Flight Crew involves some degree of self-discipline and perhaps a change in behaviour. In any dealings with Core managers or Activators they must strenuously avoid offering *any* encouragement to revert to the old ways. Instead they must take every opportunity to reinforce the new ones. This may sound simple and rather obvious but it is surprising how often it is missed.

Lastly, there are the Activators themselves, who should be encouraged to forge new impromptu, cross-functional networks. The workshops provide one opportunity and so too do the learning sets we discuss in Chapter 6. However, yet again, one of the keys to success is the attitude of the Core. There seems to be a difference here between the desire often expressed by managers for their staff to be more independent and resourceful, and their reaction when such a state of affairs actually comes about. In fact, we have even had managers effectively complaining that the process they asked for is going rather too well. They get upset when, instead of coming to them for help, Activators pick up the phone or use e-mail to talk to one of their peers. They feel excluded and maybe even a little threatened. Fortunately, when this happens it is a sign of success, and is relatively easily fixed by the Flight Crew refocusing the manager concerned on the high status elements of their new role, like strategic planning and coaching, which they may temporarily have lost sight of.

So when it comes to supporting the programme, everyone should be involved in one way or another. It is this highly inclusive quality which gives this design one of its advantages over more conventionally-structured training and development. It is the responsibility of everyone to take every opportunity to reinforce the use of the new language, behaviours and processes, even down to good naturedly catching one another when old habits creep back in.

System support in this case relates to the mechanisms that are built into the programme design. These take a variety of forms. Some are intended to be highly responsive to events taking place within the organization, such as changing priorities and crises. Others must of necessity behave in ways which are very robust and *in*flexible, some people have even suggested unreasonable, in the face of largely the same pressures. Perhaps this latter group needs some explanation. What it all boils down to is how important the programme is or is not in the overall scheme of things. If it is genuinely perceived as having an important role to play in the journey towards healthier social capital then it must be protected from diversions. Otherwise, for example, the timing of modules becomes negotiable, gaps appear and the momentum is lost. Once lost, it is very difficult to recover. New, still fragile, ways of working essential to the development of healthier social capital are left bare and unsupported as organizational attention moves temporarily onto another priority. They don't last long against the powerful competition of other work demands. Indeed, if the programme is going to hit a rough patch, as at some time it undoubtedly will, this is one of the first places to look for the cause and to take the corrective action. The mechanisms for system support are described in the last section of this chapter.

The pay-offs

Obviously there have to be enough valued pay-offs to justify the investment in this kind of design. In addition to the economic and bottom line related ones of the type illustrated by the UDV example, here are some other good reasons why this approach should commend itself.

The programme design offers a strong benefit from cross-fertilization and network building which helps break down barriers, enhance understanding and a sense of oneness. When people begin to take time to understand each other's problems and priorities it is much more difficult to endow them with horns and demonize them. They develop a sense of perspective about their own problems and priorities and see them in the context of the wider operation. They see ways they can contribute of which they had previously been unaware.

In order to maximize impact and to avoid the dilution effect associated with piecemeal training, this programme is designed to create a critical mass of people who are all going through the same learning experience at the same time. It engenders an environment which is friendly to the experimentation and personal risk taking so necessary for the efficient adoption of any new behaviour by a large group of people. It also greatly encourages the development of new language and conventions which apply in a climate of healthy social capital and assists their speedy adoption through common usage and daily reinforcement. Indeed the common use of new language and conventions acts to spread the influence of the programme far beyond the boundaries of those who are actually participating in it and in so doing embraces all employees.

Because learning is focused on practical and real work issues, it is much easier to evaluate the impact of this kind of programme than those with a looser structure and less defined applications. There is a real connection with performance and with day-to-day tasks. At Activator level the pay-offs are often quick if not immediate. People feel they are actually getting somewhere and the organization measures confirm it. The organization feels like it is a success. It feels worth belonging to.

Another pay-off comes from the amount of creativity and energy released by involvement in the process. New unsuspected talent emerges. Dormant performers become dynamic. Those who do not want to play, stand out clearly for everyone to see, allowing their swift removal. The best people can be retained in satisfying jobs without feeling the necessity to seek promotion within the organization or alternative work elsewhere – an increasingly vexatious issue for today's flatter organizations.

It is not too difficult to see how these developments would benefit an *organization* which has set itself on the road to developing healthier social capital, but what is in it for individual members? Behavioural change is often neither easy nor comfortable. Some people do not see why they should have to bother. After all, they have made it through life reasonably successfully so far. Others would like to change, but are fearful of what people might say and perhaps have doubts about their ability to change successfully. These fears and reservations must be properly addressed. There must be valued pay-offs for individuals as well as for the community or it just won't happen. Activators who have participated in past programmes have offered the following thoughts about the pay-offs they experienced:

- much better relationships across functional and, where applicable, geographical boundaries;
- more productive relationships with Flight Crew;
- a feeling of personal growth and the realization of potential as greater skill in interpersonal transactions produces better outcomes;
- real role clarity;
- a greater feeling of belonging and support;
- improved personal performance and the feel-good factor which attends it;
- an often undreamt expansion of personal and career horizons;
- an increased sense of independence and adventure.

The pitfalls

There is always the potential for things to go wrong and it is as well to know what they are in advance.

In most organizations there are inevitably problems releasing people for training. In order to get round these and turn the situation to advantage, the programme is structured in tranches, each of which should be composed of individuals drawn from different functions, and, if applicable, from different sites. As well as the powerful cross-border networks this creates, it means that no one unit is depleted drastically by workshop attendance at any one time. The short duration of workshops in each module also assists in minimizing the disruption as well as maximizing the beneficial impact.

As we suggested on p. 112, some managers do not see the training and development of their people as central to their role. They see it instead as a function for HR. If that is acceptable, then this kind of programme is not for your organization. If it is unacceptable some education will naturally be required along with the winning of the hearts and minds.

The shared journey concept makes real demands on the time and energy of Core managers and Flight Crew. If the other demands on the time of these people mean that support can only ever be half-hearted at best, then it is better not to start than to start and falter.

Lastly, while the Activators can be a rich source of practical ideas and are of undoubted importance to present and future performance, we have never seen them as drivers of culture change. This makes Activator level a poor place to start. So, if your organization finds itself right at the beginning of the journey, there are other actions which will pay their dividends earlier, as the tactical positioning guide on pp. 193–6 indicates.

Summary

These pitfalls notwithstanding, there are significant arguments for including the Activators on the journey towards healthy social capital. Doing so can free up managers at higher levels to engage in work more appropriate to their talents and salaries and can make the most of the resources and talents of all. The programme can be highly cost-effective in delivering major performance improvements on real work tasks and hence the bottom line. And lastly, its highly inclusive approach is entirely consistent with the sense of commitment and belonging so essential to the creation of an environment rich in healthy social capital.

Checklist

This checklist focuses on the principal features and broad practicalities of the programme design raised in the second section of this chapter and is offered as an aid to assessing their relevance to your organization. Try it now or skip till later as you wish.

In my organization:

There is a strong feeling of energy and excitement about the   I Agree/I Disagree
training and development (T&D) experience.

T&D activities are seen as focused on what is important.	I Agree/I Disagree
T&D activities feel like a shared journey. Everyone gets involved.	I Agree/I Disagree
The real development happens in the real work environment.	I Agree/I Disagree
There is no significant burn up on re-entry to the workplace.	I Agree/I Disagree
Core manager support is given immediately on return from a workshop.	I Agree/I Disagree
Application plans are focused on areas where real operational value-add can be obtained.	I Agree/I Disagree
Core managers see the drive to develop Activators as a worthwhile investment of their time and energy.	I Agree/I Disagree
The Flight Crew actively reinforce new behaviours and discourage reversion to old ways.	I Agree/I Disagree
Peer support back in the workplace is an important and valuable feature of T&D activity.	I Agree/I Disagree
The impact of T&D activities are not diluted or diverted by other apparently more urgent pressures and priorities.	I Agree/I Disagree
T&D activities are seen as very responsive to changing business priorities.	I Agree/I Disagree
T&D activities are very effective at breaking down any functional and factional boundaries that exist and promoting collective effectiveness.	I Agree/I Disagree
T&D activities encourage people to take a wider perspective and think of the needs of the whole organization.	I Agree/I Disagree
The effects of T&D are actively encouraged to spread spontaneously.	I Agree/I Disagree
It is easy to see and evaluate the impact of T&D on performance.	I Agree/I Disagree
T&D stimulates dormant performers and exposes those who will not or cannot play.	I Agree/I Disagree
T&D contains valued personal pay-offs for those participating.	I Agree/ I Disagree
Releasing people to participate in T&D workshops is not a problem.	I Agree/ I Disagree
T&D activities produce real and immediate improvements in ways of working and create new norms.	I Agree/ I Disagree

We do not really need a critical mass of Activators who understand and are fully committed to the organization's objectives in order to achieve present and future success.	I Agree/I Disagree
We are already making the most of the Activator resources (actual and potential) which results in Core managers being able to devote their time to work which is more consistent with their talents and salaries.	I Agree/I Disagree

If you either answered Disagree or perhaps wished there was a 'maybe' category, then a programme of the type we describe for the Activators may make a significant difference to the introduction of healthier social capital in your organization, as well as improving its overall performance.

The detail of the programme

The following pages describe the process for setting up and running a modular programme which will help in achieving healthy social capital as well as enhancing short, medium and long-term business performance. The design is also ideal for the development of interpersonal skills and ways of working necessary for the introduction of the Key Interactions process, described in Chapter 2.

Laying the foundations

Ensure top level commitment

Both the Navigator and the Flight Crew must understand the commitment they are making and believe that it is worthwhile. Prior to the start of the programme, some vital work usually needs to be done to ensure that everyone at the top level understands what participating will really mean for *them*. It is particularly important that they see and are convinced of the benefits for them personally.

There must be a champion for the programme who is enough of a big hitter to carry the rest of the Flight Crew with him or her. The choice of champion is vitally important. It is always tempting to select the Navigator and indeed this may work sometimes. However, the qualities which make the Navigator effective in their inspirational role are not always the same as those that make an effective programme champion. For instance, no matter how passionate on the subject at the start, will the Navigator still be paying enough attention to the detail as the programme rolls out over the following months? Our experience of this has been mixed and so we might lean toward recommending a senior and high status member of the Flight Crew.

The champion and any other Flight Crew that will be affected must meet on a sufficient number of occasions to ensure full understanding of the programme, its objectives and their personal responsibilities. They must be prepared to buy into the disciplines of the programme and understand the pain, both organizational and personal, that so doing will generate from time to time.

Engage the Core managers

Preparation is one of the keys to success. Core managers must be fully equipped to act as supporters and coaches.

An assessment should be carried out of Core managers' state of readiness to fulfil the vital role they have in this kind of programme. They must be able to identify and then adopt an appropriate style to suit their people both individually and collectively and they must be able to change that style over time as their people grow. They must also be able to help their people with the creation of behavioural application plans which are specific and relevant, which are stretching but achievable and the results of which can be objectively assessed once they are completed. These are widely referred to as Specific, Measurable, Achievable, Realistic and Time-bound (SMART) objectives, the creation of which is a skill more often admitted to than present. Where this skill is not present it must be acquired. Above all, Core managers must be equipped with sound coaching skills and be adept in negotiating high-quality performance deals with their staff (see the Field of Freedom pp. 101–2).

Establish a Steering Group and get approval for the starting subjects

The Steering Group should be chaired by a member of the Flight Crew or, in the event of a very large organization, the senior unit manager or operational director (in person, not a convenient deputy) – an important signal. Other members should include two or three Core managers who may change as the programme progresses, a senior representative from HR and the programme tutors. Selected Activators can also provide a useful perspective, but care must be taken in their selection to avoid accusations of elitism or favouritism.

The first task of the Steering Group is to develop the timescales for the first twelve months and to select the subjects for the first four to five modules for approval by the Flight Crew or champion. Thereafter as the programme moves along, the Steering Group will meet at least once per module to:

- oversee and sign off each step of the programme ensuring it is delivering its objectives;
- continually sample the environment so that module subjects selected reflect current business priorities, whilst maintaining a coherent and rational development path and a shape and flow which is discernible and logical for the participants;
- challenge any cosy thinking about how well the programme is going;

- troubleshoot and ring early warning bells when things try to start going wrong;
- continuously and actively seek out evidence of how the programme is affecting behaviour and performance;
- actively promote the aims of the programme and emphasize its relevance at every opportunity;
- flag up successes for prominent recognition.

Starting the programme

The programme should have a specific start date which applies to all participants. The timing is important as the aim is to embark all concerned on a shared journey and thus create a critical mass of people all of whom are engaged in using new behaviours and ways of working. We favour a simple launch date announcement with the pre-launch activities and the level of Navigator and Flight Crew support speaking for the importance and significance of the programme rather than a high-profile launch event. However, if conventions dictate otherwise, then so be it.

It is certainly true that some understanding must be achieved across the organization as regards what the programme is about and the way it is designed to work. So the announcement or whatever must contain sufficient information to achieve this along with a genuinely two-way clarification process which offers the opportunity for people to have their questions answered.

In addition to this general two-way communication exercise, the Activators and their Core managers need a more intensive and detailed preparation. This usually takes the form of familiarization or orientation sessions. A one-day session is the norm for Activators, but the Core managers may require more, depending on their development level in relation to the key interpersonal skills they will need to support the programme effectively. Both types of session are delivered prior to the start of the programme proper.

By the end of a typical one-day familiarization session for Activators, they should:

- understand the purpose and expected outcomes of the programme;
- know what the overall programme looks like, what has to be done and when;
- be familiar with any supporting materials which may be provided, such as workbooks and application plans, and how they work;
- understand and buy into the commitments involved in actively participating;
- know what support they can expect;

- understand the responsibilities of a member of a learning set, if appropriate;
- have discussed the benefits and relevance of the programme to their job and to performance targets;
- have raised, discussed and dealt with any foreseeable barriers or issues;
- be aware of the focus of the first module and have begun to consider the content of that module and possible future modules.

For Core managers, the content is broadly similar, with the addition of some debate about their role in supporting the Activators and whatever skills practice is required. The duration can range from one day to several, the latter being applicable if, for instance, the skill base for a key function like coaching were not well developed. Skills practice will also need to include negotiating Fields of Freedom and setting SMART objectives if this or a similar process is unfamiliar to the Core managers.

Running the programme proper – the essential components

The Shape and Flow

To illustrate where each of the components lies, here is an example of the first 28 weeks (three modules) of a single tranche programme of 12–16 people, after all the general communication and orientation sessions have taken place.

Week 0	Preparatory sessions to familiarize Core managers with module 1 material
Week 1	2-day workshop for the first module subject
Weeks 1 and 2	Activators prepare first SMART behavioural application plans
Week 3	Core managers and Activators meet to agree SMART behavioural application plans
Weeks 4–11	Activators put application plans into practice with appropriate support from their Core managers
Week 8	Preparatory session to familiarize Core managers with module 2 material
Week 9	2-day workshop for second module subject
Weeks 9 and 10	Activators prepare SMART behavioural application plans
Week 11	Core managers and Activators meet to agree SMART behavioural application plans for module 2 and to review progress on their module 1 application plans

Weeks 12–19	Activators put application plans into practice with appropriate support from their Core managers
Week 16	Preparatory session to familiarize Core managers with module 3 material
Week 17	2-day workshop for module 3 subject
Week 17 and 18	Activators prepare SMART behavioural application plans
Week 19	Core managers and Activators meet to agree SMART behavioural application plans for module 3 and to review progress on previous application plans
Weeks 20–27	Activators put application plans into practice with appropriate support from their Core managers
Week 24	Preparatory session to familiarize Core managers with module 4 material

In week 25 the fourth module would begin and the pattern would repeat until the programme is complete.

Deciding the programme content and order

In a modular programme it is essential that the order of the modules makes sense as well as reflecting the business priorities, existing and emerging. For instance:

- early modules may focus for the most part on the generic inter-personal skills which form the foundation for virtually all business transactions;
- as the programme progresses into module 4 and beyond, specific skills which reflect the business priorities, such as perhaps, customer focus or project management may be injected;
- at certain stages in the programme it is often useful to introduce a module such as 'Improving Financial Understanding' to provide a clearer context for the application of the new behaviours;
- towards the end of the programme, it can be a good investment of time to focus the participants on how they will continue their own development after the programme is over.

It is essential that everyone involved can readily see that the programme is building in a purposeful and coherent manner towards the fulfilment of the desired outcomes. Module subjects from past programmes include:

- Allocating work effectively
- Coaching people to think for themselves
- Collective effectiveness in modern organizations
- Contracting with colleagues
- Creativity and innovation
- Developing individuals to perform
- Developing yourself
- Effective management and what it means
- Effective written communications
- Handling difficult situations
- Interviewing for recruitment, discipline
- Introducing learning sets
- Leadership today and emotional intelligence
- Managing change
- Negotiating market deals with colleagues
- Practical health and safety
- Problem solving and decision making
- Project management in a matrix organization
- Strategic thinking
- The impact of finance on your job
- Understanding and managing your resources
- Verbal communications including engaging groups
- You and your customer (internal and external).

Prescribed time windows

These are a key component. They are essential to maintain the momentum of the programme in the face of the many powerful business pressures which threaten it. Core managers are asked to commit to meeting their Activators one to one, within a prescribed week during each module, for application planning and progress review. Once made, the commitment is considered non-negotiable. The importance of this signal cannot be overstressed. As soon as you start to allow negotiation to take place on the mechanisms, such as timing and duration of modules, in order to, say, avoid a busy period and peak holiday weeks, you can say goodbye to momentum. Of course this is difficult, and there will certainly be genuine arguments for slowing the programme, or causing it to pause. If you cannot envisage resisting all but the most exceptional of these pressures, don't start the programme.

Application planning and progress review meetings

These meetings, one per module, have a significant coaching flavour, being focused on discrete tasks and the specific behaviours necessary to carry them out successfully. They typically last an hour, but may be very much shorter if coaching skills are good and the relationship between manager and Activator is open.

SMART application plans

We use the term application rather than action to indicate that activities deriving from the modular work must be focused on the application of the learning to real and pressing work situations and the delivery of tangible value-add. That may seem to be stating the obvious, but our experience suggests that Activators and their managers are often tempted to treat action plans deriving from workshops as somehow extraneous to real work. This must be discouraged.

Activators are expected to deliver on at least one application plan per module. However, the selection of the application plan should be driven by work needs and not by the subject of the most recent module. The aim is, module by module, to build up a toolbox of practical behaviours which they use as a matter of course. Hence, by the time the programme has reached module 6, for example, an Activator's latest application plan may contain behavioural elements (tools) from a number of modules.

Workshops

Each module is supported by a workshop. Typically, workshops are of two days duration, but may be varied to suit. For example, some subjects benefit from a one-day–gap–one-day approach and on rare occasions we have used a two-day–gap–two-day approach.

A very few, like 'Coaching people to think for themselves', where a reasonably good command of the skills is required to ensure a successful re-entry to the workplace, may benefit from three consecutive days, but we strongly suggest that three days is the maximum.

Where there is likely to be significant benefit from comparing notes on the experience with fellow Activators, it can be worthwhile building in a 'follow-up' session to the next module's workshop.

The primary aim of the workshops is to expose the Activators to new ideas and best practices, to stimulate debate and argument, to get people thinking about the new ways and what they mean, as well as trying out new and often uncomfortable behaviours in a safe environment. The process of embedding the new ways however, should take place in the real world and be fully supported by the Core managers in their coaching role. In this way the behaviours, skills and attitudes necessary for the development of healthy social capital are quickly incorporated into the behavioural tool kits of a critical mass of individuals.

Preparatory sessions for managers

In order for Core managers to be able to fully and energetically support the behavioural development and continuous improvement in task effectiveness of their Activators, they must be fully conversant with the content and thrust of the modules. Short preparatory sessions held immediately prior to the Activators' workshops achieve this, where frankly other methods do not. They fall into the category of a prescribed time-window activity.

In addition to acquainting Core managers with the subject matter of the upcoming module, so that coaching conversations are brief and meaningful, they also address the kind of fears and concerns discussed in Chapter 4 and so help to reduce opposition and increase co-operation from this quarter.

Support

Support comes from informal relationships developed within the participating group, learning sets (discussed in Chapter 6), the programme tutors, and naturally the Core manager acting as coach and mentor. The development of appropriate support relationships is encouraged throughout the programme and is seen as a major spin-off benefit, both in the development of individuals and in enhancing business performance. The UDV programme is a fine example. The existence of strong support networks encourages people to understand, accept the realities of, and actively manage, their working environment.

Workbooks

Using workbooks to support the programme has its plusses and minuses. On the plus side, they cater rather well for a different learning-style preference than that offered in most workshop activities, providing a structured vehicle for reflection. On the minus side, they are time consuming for the Activators, some of whom resent the intrusion into their personal time and for some populations, they carry the unpleasant whiff of study and school. If you are going to use them, it is usually best to offer Activators hints about how to get the most out of the experience, particularly if some of them have had limited formal education and therefore potentially undeveloped study skills. They are not, in our view, a substitute for workshops. However, used selectively, they can add a useful dimension to a modular programme.

Evaluation

A modular programme spread over many months must be capable of responding quickly to business needs, changes in priority and new initiatives within the wider company environment. It must also carry its own diagnostic process, so that it continually challenges any assumption that everything is going well.

Evaluation should not be left till the end. It should begin at the design stage and continue throughout. Not only does this make the final evaluation easier; it provides much valuable information about how things are going, so that the programme can be constantly improved to provide more positive impact.

The evaluation process is best run by the Steering Group who should decide what information will be gathered, collect and assess it, and consult with the Flight Crew at appropriate stages to ensure the programme is meeting expectations. Information can come from Activators on the style and content of the workshops, their application plans and progress reviews, success stories about real achievements in the workplace, Core managers and business performance measures.

Overview

During the whole of the journey it is essential that everyone keeps their eye on the overall objective. There is always the danger that programmes such as this develop a life and a purpose of their own, and this must not happen. This is an integrated, inclusive and modular programme which uses momentum and a sense of a journey shared by all to achieve a critical mass of new ways of working and so deliver a rounded environment rich in healthy social capital alongside improvements in productivity and bottom-line performance.

Chapter 6

Tapping the geyser

*Geyser – a powerful release of energy previously trapped
beneath the surface*

Here I am, brain the size of a planet and all they give me to do is ...
Marvin the depressed robot
DOUGLAS ADAMS' *HITCH-HIKERS GUIDE TO THE GALAXY*

One of the big pay-offs from investing in healthier social capital has to be
that organizations get more out of their people. That is what this chapter is
about. Not squeezing or forcing or extracting the best, but creating the
conditions where people give more of themselves than you ask and
sometimes surprise themselves by giving more than they think they have
got. The following is a real example.

At the very end of a modular programme of the type described in
Chapter 5, one of the participants was facilitating a small group in a
learning set. Having nothing better to do, now that they had essentially
worked themselves out of a job, our consultant began to muse upon the
changes which had taken place over the two years that the programme had
run. Then it suddenly occurred that the scene he was witnessing was so
dramatically different as to be quite astounding. It was only that opportunity for a short period of reflection that brought the enormity of the change
home. Otherwise the extent of the change would have been masked by its
incremental nature over the two years. Because, what came into the consultant's mind, was a picture of the now facilitator in the very first
workshop, apparently near death as a result of the torture he was undergoing. The task at that time was nothing much more than telling a group of
colleagues a bit about himself. The full colour video of the memory
returned. Was it possible for someone to show a ghostly pallor and an

unhealthy flush simultaneously, to stammer whole sentences while drinking a litre of water? Apparently so, and yet now our graduating facilitator was explaining to one of his clients about where they might be on the learning curve and making appropriate interventions in a learning set of his peers. The stigma of schooldays untouched by any form of academic success whatsoever, which the participant had carried for all of his adult life so far, seemed somehow less important now. That is what we mean by tapping the geyser!

If organizations can do that for their people, if they can give them the opportunity and the means to grow and be more than they thought possible, then surely the new deal is better than the old, even if the road to get there can sometimes be less than comfortable. If, for example, loyalty emerges, then it will not be the dependency flavoured loyalty of before, but will be based instead, on an exchange of valued contributions and founded on respect.

The ultimate aim is to engage people in the development of healthier social capital and create an organism which is robust, self-sustaining and self-improving, where self-interest and a sense of belonging rub along together in ways which extract the best from both: where people want to spend their time: where they feel they belong to a community of common interest: where they can achieve individual success as part of the whole: and where they are prepared to contribute the best of themselves.

This chapter is a bit different in construction to the others. If you like, it is a toolbox containing six different tools you can use to support and encourage the introduction of healthier social capital.

We have called the chapter, 'Tapping the geyser' because each of the tools can be employed to help release the latent power, talent and energy which exists below the surface of the human resources of many organizations.

Each of the six can be adopted individually to meet a specific organizational need, or in combination with others, for a greater effect on the critical mass of ways of working. The six are:

1   The role of coach in helping people to think for themselves and to take appropriate action;

2   The role of facilitator in supporting Key Interactions, one-to-one contracting, market deal negotiations, learning sets, and general project working;

3   A method of contracting to enable an individual to reach an agreement with a key colleague on better, more effective, more efficient ways of working;

4   A method of negotiating market deals where the complexity of the situation, or the number of interested parties, or the scope and implications of the subject, dictate a more formal process than simple contracting;

5   A behavioural template for confronting issues and handling some forms of conflict productively;

6   An introduction to the function, purpose and value-add of learning sets in the context of social capital.

One etymologically challenged individual suggested we should include a seventh item to deal with how to borrow money from an elderly gent, but it proved to be a misunderstanding about the title of the chapter. If you are similarly confused, sorry.

The role of coach in developing social capital

You could easily be forgiven for saying to yourself something like, 'Oh no, not coaching again! It seems I've been hearing about that at almost every management course I've attended for years.' So you will be relieved that we are not going to spend a lot of time listing and describing the skills and behaviours necessary for effective coaching.

If you have managers whose behavioural toolbox has a few gaps in the coaching section, there is some very good training around, although we suggest that you go for a design which majors on practice rather than theory. For example, we find that good results come from an intensive 3 day workshop focused heavily on repeated practice, observation and reflection, followed some 6 to 8 weeks thereafter by a follow-up day where participants review progress, learning, successes and setbacks with their peers.

The role of coach, specific to social capital, is focused on creating a working environment where people constantly stretch themselves both in the way they think about the tasks they are responsible for and in the way they tackle them. Coaching in this context is not therefore so much about skill development, as about attitude of mind and behaviour.

The product of the process should be people who are willing and able to think better for themselves, who make sounder judgements, who are prepared to take a few more calculated risks, who admit openly when these don't come off, and who learn from the experience. These people should possess an ever expanding repertoire of behaviours to choose from so that their day-to-day interactions with colleagues constantly act to build bit by bit, towards a state of healthy social capital.

In order to bring this about the coach will have a number of roles within the coach/coachee relationship. The following are shown in no particular order because the process is inevitably an iterative one.

1   The coach must be a good diagnostician. They must be able to assess the state of readiness of an individual for a proposed task so that the experience is stretching, not breaking. Whilst it is a truism that we

learn more from our mistakes than our successes, the effective coach must never forget the motivating power of success. By all means ask, as some bold souls suggest, 'Are you making enough mistakes?' but make sure there are some opportunities along the way for people to feel good about themselves as well. Through success comes enhanced self-esteem, sense of identity and confidence.

2   The coach must be a good sounding board. People must feel able to come to the coach for help knowing that they will not be given a solution or made to feel inadequate. If they think that, they just don't come. It is perhaps the primary reason why the ever-popular 'open door' policy has such little impact beyond the salving of the particular managerial conscience, those who choose to take advantage of the offer once, often feeling a sense of inadequacy and declining to repeat the experience. The sounding board experience should be challenging but profitable, with the coachee leaving the session feeling good about themselves and about the way forward.

3   The coach's reflective role should not be limited to the auditory either. One of their tasks is to hold up a mirror for the coachee to see themselves in action. The coach therefore must have the necessary detachment to listen to the coachee and then, through a combination of questioning, summarising and confronting, to help the coachee see the consequences of their current behaviour choices. Having gained acceptance, the pair can then work together to devise better behavioural strategies for the future.

4   Because behavioural change is often incremental in nature, successes and even significant breakthroughs can often be missed by the coachee. It must be a part of the coach's role to provide support and encouragement by bringing these to the attention of the coachee and celebrating them.

5   The coach is not a problem solver, an adviser, an instructor or an expert. Their task is to help people think for themselves and so tap the geyser and release the buried potential; and that in itself produces a tension. While the process is rightly focused on real and current tasks, with their imperatives for short- and medium-term solutions, the other significant goal is to develop the potential of the coachee in ways which will maximize their future contribution to the success of the organization. The effective coach is able to manage the tension between the need for rapid solutions and the inevitably slower process of development.

6   Where behaviour needs improvement, the coach must be able to confront the unproductive or inappropriate behaviour, without producing a defensive reaction from the coachee. This kind of coaching is often avoided by coaches until the problem behaviour becomes quite serious. Time saving, the reason often given, is a false economy, albeit an understandable one, but it is not usually just that. Confronting someone's behaviour is harder than confronting a skill deficiency; it can feel a lot more personal to both parties. The coach needs a tool to make a successful outcome more likely. We offer one on p.156.

7   The coach must not become so enthralled with the role that they lose sight of the fact that a good return is required from the investment. It is important therefore that coaches don't try to coach the uncoachable. If the assessment of an individual is that the time and effort required for a successful result would be disproportionate to the benefit gained, the individual should either be left to get on with it or more drastic surgical action taken.

In summary, all this is not easy for the coach. They are required to relinquish control in favour of influence, focus on the nuances of behaviour where cause and effect are often more relevant than right and wrong, have the self-discipline and courage to allow the coachee to learn from their mistakes and grow in strength and ability without interference and have the good judgement to know when to step in. Engaging the latent potential of the organization's resources can be a scary feeling. And the loss of hands-on control of day-to-day events in favour of arm's-length influencing is not the only novel experience for managers who become coaches. The change from pushing people to do things, into being alert to the need to step in with challenging questions when they are in danger of going too far, is a fundamental one which can often feel personally threatening for the new coach on their early learning curve. Who then will coach the coach? The Flight Crew of course!

The return for the investment is to free up coach–managers to fulfil their own potential by allowing them to concentrate more on strategy, leadership and the orchestration of their resources than the operational preoccupations of the day.

For the coachee, who is asked to stretch and use intellectual and emotional muscles which may not have been used before and who may be asked to radically re-examine their way of looking at working life, the pay-offs include better ways of working, more satisfying work, more responsibility and a greater sense of belonging and worth.

For both roles, the ultimate pay-off is to be part of an organization which seeks to maximize the contributions of its people, and helps them grow to become self-reliant, high performers in an environment where individual and collective achievement are complementary.

Checklist

You may find this checklist helpful to assess the degree to which coaching, as described in the foregoing section, currently exists within your organization.

In my organization:

The focus on coaching extends well beyond skills to include attitude of mind and behaviour.	I Agree/I Disagree
Coaching has produced a critical mass of behaviours which is taking us bit by bit towards a working environment rich in healthy social capital.	I Agree/I Disagree
The coaching process is building self-esteem, a sense of identity and confidence.	I Agree/I Disagree
Coaches are good at assessing the state of readiness of an individual so that the experience is stretching, not breaking.	I Agree/I Disagree
The focus of coaching is as much about future development as the task in hand.	I Agree/I Disagree
Coaches use good judgement to know when to step in and when to let the coachee grow from the whole experience.	I Agree/I Disagree
Coaches are well equipped to confront coachee behaviour without causing defensive responses.	I Agree/I Disagree
Coaches don't waste time on coaching the uncoachable.	I Agree/I Disagree
Coaches have already freed themselves up through the medium of coaching to concentrate on higher level tasks.	I Agree/I Disagree
Coaches are widely perceived as sources of support and encouragement.	I Agree/I Disagree
Coaches already show great self-discipline in adopting the role of influencer and surrendering the role of hands-on controller.	I Agree/I Disagree
Coaches use the motivating power of success to build confidence and self-esteem in the coachee.	I Agree/I Disagree
Coaches are excellent questioners, listeners and sounding boards.	I Agree/I Disagree

Coaches are skilled at holding up a mirror for the coachees to see their own behaviour.	I Agree/I Disagree
Coaches are skilled in using helping tools and processes including confronting and problem solving.	I Agree/I Disagree
Coaches are a major force in tapping the geyser.	I Agree/I Disagree

If you either answered Disagree or perhaps wished there was a 'maybe' category, then some action on coaching is required in order to be able to introduce and sustain an environment of healthy social capital.

The role of facilitator in developing social capital

One of the arguments we continually make in this book is that healthy social capital demands the replacement of partisan and factional gain as an objective with a commitment to achieving outcomes which are in the best interests of the organization as a whole. All organizations would claim that is exactly what they are set up to do *now* of course, and who would want to argue. Yet, in our experience, we find that there is often a considerable difference between the intent and the practice on the ground, where relationships within groups and between functions can often be epitomized by poorly synchronized goals, political manoeuvring, mutual suspicion and even hostility.

The same kind of discrepancy also exists between organizations' natural desire to extract the most from their human resource, and the reality where much of the talent and energy is allowed to remain at best poorly focused and at worst untapped.

To help counteract these common dysfunctions, we suggest the role of specialist facilitator, a title oft misunderstood, even shrouded in some mystique. In fact, the role is quite simple in concept and yet extremely demanding in practice, if it is done well. Perhaps that is why the mystique exists!

In Chapter 4, we described coaching as a game all the family should play, but facilitating as a more specialized function with fewer practitioners. It is not in fact necessary or even advisable for every manager to become one, even though some skills are common to both roles. Indeed, there will be some who either cannot or will not adopt the degree of detachment necessary for the role to succeed.

The facilitator's job is to help develop healthier social capital by improving the effectiveness of the way people work together *in groups*. Their role is to:

- support the development of micro-environments where people openly share issues and problems with certain peers and utilize the rich pool of knowledge, experience, skill and attitude, to find the best way to progress specific ideas, problems and projects (see learning sets on p.159);

- act as a catalyst when groups get stuck in bad rituals and behaviours and need some kind of breakthrough to be able to move forward.
- ease the passage of difficult, particularly cross-border, incidents;
- observe, surface and confront dysfunctional behaviour which is impacting on the ability of any group to deliver the best they can;
- mediate, that is to say, interpose themselves between parties as a friend to each;
- offer a process, and when it is accepted, take charge of that process;
- work with project groups that are encountering barriers to progress; These groups may be formally constituted under a project title, or they may be informal collections of interested parties which have formed more or less spontaneously and of their own accord to address a problem, issue or idea of collective interest. These kind of groups are most common in a matrix-type organization, an environment very compatible with healthy social capital.

In all cases, the facilitator exists to create the conditions where positive things happen. To achieve this, they must be able to stay detached from the subject matter of the meeting. That is to say, they should not have an outcome in mind or a partisan view themselves which they have a vested interest in promoting. For this reason, it is inappropriate for the facilitator to be the manager or an interested member of the group. Instead, facilitators should be masters of process. They will watch and know when to intervene and when not to. They will focus on how the behaviour and attitudes within the group are helping or hindering progress, and what needs to change in order for the task or objectives to be met effectively and efficiently. In this, they may be very prescriptive once their clients have developed respect for their value-add. In order to maximize that value-add, both facilitator and client group must be clear about the role and this should be contracted for at the outset of any relationship, so that the facilitator has a license to practise.

Introducing specialist facilitators

The route to facilitation, we suggest, is this. First, people must understand the value-add the role offers and how to make the most effective use of it: so some quality communication is required at the outset. Specifically, it is important for both practitioners and clients to understand that the skills are generic and can be of benefit in any setting, regardless of the task at hand. Second, facilitators should be selected using something like the following person profile.

Facilitators should either have already, or should have the potential to develop:

- a sound working knowledge of the organization. There is a large difference between asking quality questions that help the client think something through, and taking up the client's time with requests for information which only illuminate the facilitator's lack of background understanding and serve to reduce both their effectiveness and their standing;
- a clear understanding and acceptance of the Navigator's vision and its practical implication for ways of working;
- an understanding of what social capital means in practice;
- an ability to keep the group's task and objectives in view and to tailor active involvement, such as process suggestions or interventions, to improve the group dynamic to that end. Sometimes facilitators can go native and start practising their art for its own sake. Where it occurs this must be stopped;
- a degree of independence and self-reliance;
- an ability to establish rapport with individuals and groups even in difficult circumstances;
- a repertoire of skills such as listening and questioning;
- an ability to challenge without alienating;
- an ability to confront issues without provoking a defensive response;
- the self-discipline to observe for long periods without speaking;
- the determination to probe where necessary even, on occasion, against some opposition;
- a small tool kit of processes such as problem solving, to inject when necessary and the self-restraint to leave well alone when not. Always a tricky judgement call;
- the strength of character to contract for the full range of facilitator involvement at the outset and to resist any overtures from clients to 'just take the minutes as well while you are here!'

Training facilitators

Training facilitators can take some time. Much depends on the skill base those selected are starting from. The training should be provided by someone with experience, as the learning process can be personally challenging, and, if handled inappropriately by the trainer, even potentially damaging.

Where learning sets are to be part of an initiative, they can provide an excellent forum for early practice, and, whenever possible, we suggest that those selected for the role should initially be employed in supporting learning set activity. This provides an opportunity for practice in the process skills required, in a controlled and structured environment, and has the added benefit of allowing facilitators to be put into sets not in the their own unit, thereby getting them used to the idea of controlling the process while remaining detached from the task outcome.

Checklist

You may find this checklist helpful to assess the degree to which partisan behaviour and under-utilized resources, as described in the foregoing section, currently exist within your organization.

In my organization:

People already openly share issues and utilize the rich resources   I Agree/I Disagree
of knowledge, skill and experience that their colleagues possess.

Groups either don't get stuck in bad rituals or have the skills to   I Agree/I Disagree
get out of them without external help.

Groups already have an effective tool kit of processes to address   I Agree/I Disagree
any issues like problem solving as they arise.

People from different functions regularly come together   I Agree/I Disagree
spontaneously to solve cross-functional conflicts and do so
effectively.

People have the interpersonal skills necessary to resolve conflicts   I Agree/I Disagree
in the best interests of the organization as a whole.

People already work together very effectively in groups.   I Agree/I Disagree

When working in groups, people put aside partisan interests in   I Agree/I Disagree
favour of the greater good.

Project groups work perfectly without the need for a non-partisan   I Agree/I Disagree
facilitator.

When people need to work collectively, they make full use of all   I Agree/I Disagree
the resources of the group.

If you either answered Disagree or perhaps wished there was a 'maybe' category, then some action on facilitating would be helpful in the drive toward healthier social capital.

Contracting for better ways of working together

Contracting is essentially a one-to-one process which offers a way of breaking through the barriers of suspicion, misunderstanding and hostility which frequently exist between units, functions and individuals at work, and delivering more efficient working methods, more effective interactions, and pleasanter working relationships. It is not about getting to know the other person intimately. For most of us, most of the time, there simply is not the opportunity or even the desire to do so. Instead, what is needed, is a process which enables any dysfunctions to be fixed in a way which brings maximum benefit to the whole organization and which employs behaviours consistent with healthier social capital.

Contracting is a process which enables individual A to tackle a situation, in which individual B's performance of a specific piece of work (or general attitude or behaviour) is causing A difficulties, and do a deal to improve things.

What might these things be? What do we really want from those key people with whom we interact and whose performance has a significant impact on our ability to do our job well, on our feelings of well-being or otherwise, on our promotion or demotion? How do we want to be treated by our colleagues? Frequently voiced aspirations, which seem to hold true across the board, regardless for instance, of position in the organization or whether the speaker happens to be the customer or the supplier in the interaction, include:

- no nasty surprises;
- being treated with courtesy and fairness;
- to work *together* to solve problems;
- to be listened to and understood;
- a positive and flexible attitude;
- easy and frequent exchange of information;
- early warning of problems;
- to be treated with respect and held in high regard;
- to be certain of easy contact and a positive response in an emergency;
- reliability;
- consistency and competence;
- to have friendly and compatible systems;
- no personal attacks;
- no games or politics;
- agreements are honoured;
- being open to ideas for improvements;
- to have questions answered.

With such commonality of experience and aspirations it may be surprising that there is a need for a contracting process at all, and yet there is. Just listen to one unit talk about another. It can sound like they come from a different planet. All sorts of malicious motives can be attributed to these aliens who, as often happens, work just down the corridor. Accusations of incompetence, which, if the accuser really stopped to think about it, would be ridiculous. Can that other unit really be completely staffed by slothful morons? If so, it presupposes a consistency in the recruitment process, which, in other circumstances, would be as admirable as it is rare.

Why then do people sometimes feel it necessary to caricature their colleagues in these unflattering and often inaccurate ways?

One cause of the problem seems to be that, at least in some measure, we are forced to accept ill-founded, uncorroborated pictures of others, because there is simply not enough time to check them out. Chance encounters, glimpses of behaviour and hearsay condition our view of those whom we do not meet frequently enough to come to know, but whom we must rely upon to help us succeed in our roles. Unfamiliarity is not the sole cause of course. The existence of some historical baggage between the parties, such as an event in the past which now colours every interaction, is another very common element. However, whilst the causes may vary, the outcomes are fairly consistent and usually not particularly beneficial to the efficient operation of the organization. What happens is that individual A adopts a behaviour based on a caricature of individual B, for any interactions with that individual. Individual B responds to this treatment in kind by either reinforcing the impression or reacting to it. Motives are assigned to behaviours by both parties and the dance of misperceptions and misdiagnoses spirals off out of control.

The feature which compounds the problem in all cases is the failure to check out just enough reality to achieve a good working relationship – and no more. If the perception exists that there is no time to address the reality of the situation, we are forced back to rely on insubstantial and partial pictures of these important, albeit essentially peripheral players in our lives. These pictures are self-perpetuating unless action is taken.

Contracting offers a focused, fast and usually painless process for tackling these situations and bringing enough reality to bear to be able to rub along. As always there are some barriers to this being a naturally occurring phenomenon. However the following real story provides an example of how the problems are much worse in the anticipation than in practice.

Illustrative example of contracting

We were running a modular programme for a client. For one of the modules (it was about module 5 or 6, so it would be roughly a year into the programme), we ran a workshop focused on contracting. We had done some data gathering, and it was apparent that there was considerable suspicion and disaffection between individuals in a number of units and functions, and that it was getting quite seriously in the way of everyone achieving their performance targets. They were very busy people. By and large, they were also very committed and able. That is not necessarily how they saw each other however. They didn't like the ways of working, but they had got used to them and they certainly had neither the time nor the inclination to sort things out on their own!

We had prepared the ground. In the previous modules, the participants had begun to acquire the skills necessary for contracting to be a success, even though most still had some way to go along the learning curve.

Before the contracting workshops, we wrote to each of the participants individually, positioning the workshop in relation to the programme so far and asking each person the following:

By (date) please let me have the names and roles of three people with whom you interact regularly and where an improvement in that interaction would make a positive difference to your performance. They should be as follows:

- one participant in the programme from your own workshop;

- one participant in the programme whom you don't normally meet at workshops who may be your manager if you so choose;

- one stranger to the programme.

You will need to explain to the people you select that inclusion means that they may be asked to give up half an hour of their time on 1 of the 2 days of the workshop to engage in a facilitated discussion with you. So please also check that you are selecting people who will be available then.

During the course of the workshop you will be asked to carry out a number of contracting sessions with some or all of these people and to come to real agreements which will be applied in the real workplace. In order to do so, you will need to employ active listening as well as the previously practised skills of assertive negotiating, planning and committing to action and to build in review milestones, opportunities for two-way feedback and contingency plans.

Your name _____   Your manager's name _____

On the day, the atmosphere was tense as the participants arrived. We began with a bit of a warm-up, touching again on the skills they would use. Lots of discussion. Some barely concealed hysteria, some not so well concealed. The first of our invited guests arrived. Never has a workshop been so still. The tension was palpable. The first sessions started. Ten minutes later, the first sessions began to conclude. Some lasted up to 20 minutes. More hysteria, but qualitatively different this time. Relief. 'Should it be that easy?' 'Yes but it won't always be.' 'Oh, OK I think I'll do another one.'

That is more or less how the workshop went. They got tired of course. New skills take it out of a person, even when they work well, and not all did. Yet enough did to convince them it was a good idea. We produced about forty agreements, if memory serves. None earth-shattering, but that wasn't the idea. Start with small successes and build. That is what works with contracting. And there were some really good agreements, most in the customer/supplier area and quite a lot of reliability and quality issues; each a small step forwards in helping deliver the goods.

The managers were on their best behaviour and where they were involved, those sessions went quite well too. The upshot was a mix of elation, relief that the contracting approaches had been well received and some frustration that, as it was so easy, they had not tried it before. Post-workshop euphoria must always be qualified of course. For a start some of it really wasn't that easy. It just felt that way when it was over and people's worst fears were not realized. And the behaviours they had learnt had also contributed towards making it seem easier than they thought it would be. And those attending were on their best behaviour and most knew at least some of the language by this time too. And the problems being aired *were* deliberately kept small. There would be tougher challenges to come. However, the agreements were real and the benefits were real, and afterwards, the practice began to spread through the fine old medium of the critical mass. We haven't been back for a year or two but the last time we popped in, the new ways had become accepted, the people were happier and they were producing significantly better performance against their key measures for far less effort. Not a bad return on investment really.

The general principles of good contracting:

1   In an environment of healthy social capital, where the object is not to win for oneself or one's unit, but rather for the organization as a whole, a successful outcome requires both parties to make the time and effort to fully understand each other's position, feelings, perspectives, needs and objectives. A light hearted, but nonetheless insightful illustration of our common failure to do so was offered by Douglas Adams's character, Slartibartfast, in *Life, the Universe and Everything*. He had a spaceship which no one else could see, not because it was invisible but because it was covered by the 'Somebody Else's Problem Field.' Contracting only works if you are prepared to see through the other person's eyes and to treat them with respect.

2   It is important not to attack the other person. As soon as you start to criticise or blame the person with whom you are about to attempt to

negotiate a contract, you create the potential for a defensive response. If, for example, you stick someone with a label like aggressive or untrustworthy, then you have moved from tackling the behaviour into attacking the person, and the chances of success are dramatically reduced. Instead the interaction becomes adversarial, a contest of wills.

3   In order to moderate any adversarial tendencies, the two negotiators should behave as if there were three entities present, not two. These are yourself, the other person and the subject you want to tackle. The aim is to enlist the other person in helping to find the best way to tackle the third entity. In this way the problem is depersonalized and becomes the rightful focus of attention.

4   To conduct the process effectively, the initiator of the contracting session must at least have some skills like assertiveness, active listening, questioning including reflecting, empathic responding, conflict handling, negotiating, rephrasing and summarizing, checking understanding and naturally they must understand the contracting process itself.

Contracting in practice

Step 1

The first thing to do in almost all instances, is to set aside a small amount of time to think, so that you can be clear about:

- the detail and facts surrounding the current state of affairs;
- how ideally you would like things to be in the short, medium and longer term;
- what kind of working relationship you need with the other person in the future to secure a good and sustainable result.

Write down a short sentence with your conclusions, so that you can remember it when things get difficult.

Step 2

Next, give some thought to how the meeting will need to run if it is to produce the outcomes you want. As you are initiating the meeting, your behaviour is likely to set the tone. You will want to choose and use the behaviours best suited to achieve your objective. All this effort may not seem fair, especially if you consider yourself to be the injured party, but being right in these circumstances can have surprisingly little bearing on the outcome. Three areas are key to producing a satisfactory outcome.

They are yourself, the other person and the subject to be discussed. You must try to analyse all three before you make any overtures towards the other person. It only takes five minutes and can save a massive amount of time and heartache.

Here are some of the questions we have found useful in helping people with this analysis.

Yourself – What do you know about yourself in this kind of situation?

- How do you act? What do you do and say?
- How do you feel about the upcoming session, going in?
- How have you behaved in similar situations in the past? In what respect was your behaviour appropriate or inappropriate?
- What is your greatest fear?
- How do you normally tackle this kind of interaction?
- What one or two behaviours can you adopt that would have the most impact in leading to your desired outcome?
- How do you want to feel after the event?
- In what frame of mind are you entering the session now that you have completed your analysis?

The other person – What do you know about them?

- How well do you know them?
- Have you ever been in this situation with them before? How did they act?
- Are their behaviours predictable or unpredictable?
- What do you think they will want out of the meeting?
- What is their usual style of behaviour? Will they need drawn out or will they be talkative? Will they be defensive, acceptant, aggressive or what?
- What will they be *thinking* about the forthcoming session?
- What do you think they will be *feeling* about the forthcoming session?
- How do you think they might describe you and their relationship with you?
- How able are they intellectually and emotionally to handle what you need to talk about?
- What effect do you think your choice of 'good' behaviours might have on them and how are they likely to respond?

The subject – What do you know about the task or problem?

- Is it complex or routine?
- On balance, who has most know-how; you or the other person? Will they see it that way?
- Is it time critical or is there plenty of time to discuss all aspects thoroughly before reaching a decision?

- Are the risks high or low? What are they?
- Are there many outcomes possible or only one?
- Has this or anything similar happened before? What took place? What was the outcome?
- Is your take on the subject likely to coincide with the other person's perspective or will they see things quite differently?

If, on reflection, you reach the conclusion that the degree of difficulty and complexity is greater than you had at first thought, it may be helpful to take a look at confronting and market deals, processes that are described later in this chapter on pp. 151 and 156. In most cases however, having prepared thoroughly, attuned your thinking to the three elements of the contracting session, and considered your objectives, you can initiate the contact.

Step 3

During the meeting you must set the tone in your initial greeting, explain the purpose as you see it clearly, being sure not to inject any accusatory note and really listen to the other person's reaction. Be open about your needs and your desire for an outcome which suits both parties. Really listen to their needs. Ask for help in finding the best solution. Make real and obvious efforts to understand how they are feeling if that is an issue, and explicitly ask them to do the same for you. None of this guarantees success, but at least if it does fail, you will both know exactly where you stand.

Step 4

When you reach a conclusion, it is imperative that you both reach the same one. Write it down. It need only be a very simple reminder and is not intended to be used as a weapon in the event of lapses. Here is one that works well.

Contract

My name _____   Your name _____

To improve our mutual effectiveness I NEED you to _____

To improve our mutual effectiveness I OFFER to _____

To achieve this I will _____   To achieve this you will _____

Signed _____   Signed _____

Checklist

You may find this checklist helpful to assess the effectiveness with which people already spontaneously tackle situations where an improvement would make a positive difference to performance.

In my organization:

Suspicion, hostility and misunderstandings do not feature in any significant way.   I Agree/I Disagree

Interactions between individuals are highly effective and show no significant dysfunctions.   I Agree/I Disagree

If any problems of quality, reliability, communication or relationship start to arise, these are dealt with immediately and effectively by the individuals concerned.   I Agree/I Disagree

There is already a recognized way in place for individuals to tackle others on performance shortcomings and it works well.   I Agree/I Disagree

When contracting with another for better performance, people always make the time and effort to understand the other person's perspective and feelings.   I Agree/I Disagree

People see problems arising from poor quality interactions as an opportunity to find an even better way to contribute to the organization's success.   I Agree/I Disagree

When raising an issue of performance with another, people as a rule take pains to confront the issue and not the person.   I Agree/I Disagree

People have the skills to contract effectively (assertiveness, listening, questioning, conflict handling) and use them frequently.   I Agree/I Disagree

When they encounter performance problems created by others, people do not rush in, but briefly analyse and plan before acting.   I Agree/I Disagree

People think about what behaviours will be effective, before they act.   I Agree/I Disagree

If you either answered Disagree or perhaps wished there was a 'maybe' category, then some action on contracting is required in order to be able to introduce and sustain an environment of healthy social capital.

Negotiating market deals

Negotiating *market deals* with colleagues is different from *contracting* in that there are often more than just two interests involved, the scope is usually greater, the costs are usually bigger and there is often more at stake. The negotiation also tends to be more formal and protracted, although not always. Many of the skills, behaviours and techniques, however, are very similar.

As we discussed in Chapters 1 and 2, market deals are important to the development of social capital because they create the *habits* which ultimately give rise to trust, or at least that working version of trust which includes reliability, respect, honesty, reputation and the like. And trust is the oil that makes the machinery glide along efficiently.

You will recall from the 'general principles' of contracting outlined on pp. 146–7 that, in an environment of healthy social capital where the object is not to win for oneself or one's unit but for the organization as a whole, a successful outcome requires negotiators to make the time and effort to fully understand the position, feelings, perspectives, needs and objectives of the other parties involved. Remember Slartibartfast? The same principle applies to market deals.

Easier said than done, however. The demands of modern organizations place a high value on action. There are plenty of other important things to be doing with our time out there. There is a sense of urgency which carries its imperative for swift decisions followed by early action. All this is very understandable but it also carries obvious dangers. It is all too easy for negotiators to succumb to the temptation to abandon the first essential parts of the market deals process far too early and get stuck into the much more familiar territory of negotiating a winning solution. What is required to prevent this unseemly haste is an explicit process which legitimizes the time spent on coming to a clear understanding *before* looking for a solution. This is a key feature of market deals.

The five stages of the process and the associated behaviour choices are

The preparation stage before the meeting

It is imperative to clarify in your own mind both what your subject goals are and the degree to which you want or need relationships to be in good working order afterwards. Prepare in advance and allow yourself some quality time to do it. Check that you have as much information as you need about the other negotiators and the subject to be discussed and be as clear as possible about the gaps in your knowledge. Also, think about your own past performance in situations like this. You may find the 'you/other(s)/subject' questions from p. 148 helpful. Bear in mind that most people spend virtually all their preparation time focusing on the subject of the negotiation, to the detriment of the outcome. When deciding on the outcomes you want from this meeting in each of the three elements of you/other(s)/subject, be very specific. Picture the door closing as the other parties leave at the conclusion of the session and look at what you have achieved.

Assuming you want to work in a way that contributes to the development of healthier social capital in your organization, give some consideration to which behaviours will be most likely to lead to you achieving your subject goals and maintaining or developing a positive working relationship for the future. Other things worth thinking about before you start are the appropriate physical environment and your true non-negotiable bottom line.

As before, this process so far should have taken no more than 5 minutes. If you need to justify that investment, think of the time it would take to put things right if you adopt the wrong strategy, or alternatively, the time you waste now working around bad deals.

The opening up stage

This is where the scene is set, the ground rules are established, the different desired outcomes discussed, and intentions made clear.

Be explicit about the process you propose and why you think it is important. Ask for agreement. Communicate your positive intentions about the nature of the outcome and future working relationships. The function of this stage is to engage the other parties in the process so that they feel it is as much theirs as yours. It takes as long as it takes. The alternative is to plough ahead without a common picture of the process that everyone is involved in and hope that it works out. That happens, but it is not pretty or effective.

The clarifying stage

The aim at this stage of any market deals session is for everyone to get a really good understanding of the different goals, perspectives and feelings represented around the table: to take time to look through other people's eyes, or walk a mile in their shoes.

This is the time to describe your desired subject and relationship outcomes in more detail and to hear other views. Be explicit and specific. Ask the others present to be the same. Show you are really listening by summarizing and asking relevant questions for clarification. Resist all temptations to debate or disagree. This is a process of non-evaluative information exchange. Be honest and open about your feelings and perceptions on the subject and encourage the others to do the same. Do not become accusatory or engage in labelling or blaming and do not in any way make any of the other negotiators into the problem. Refuse to allow anyone to make *you* the problem. Pause from time to time to take stock. Throughout, keep the subject in view on the table and treat it as the third entity in the room.

Ensure there is a common understanding of where any differences lie, which positions are negotiable and which are not. Produce a common definition of the subject which describes it accurately from all perspectives as a third entity to be tackled and solved – not as a win/lose struggle – or even a win/win one for that matter.

The generating stage

This is much more familiar ground. It involves working together to bridge any differences identified, generating options for ways forward, evaluating these options for their ability to meet all individual needs represented as well as delivering the best result for the organization as a whole. We will not dwell on the processes here as there are many effective models for problem solving and decision making around. If ideas are in short supply, however, you might consider using the Uccello Process™, which is described in Chapter 7.

The closing stage

Usually, towards the end of meetings, the world outside the door begins to make itself felt. There is a growing feeling that other things are happening out there while you are sitting here talking. There may also be some feeling of achievement – a bit of a high. People say to themselves, 'We have done well. Let's get on.' Consequently, this is a part of the meeting that tends to get rushed, with the result that some of the earlier good work may be negated.

Instead it is imperative, *before* the end of the meeting, to set aside enough time for review in order to identify and clear up any differences in perception about what has been agreed. This should be quality time, so it should not be carried out with one hand on the door handle. It is cheaper to invest a few minutes now, than it is to clear up misunderstandings which have turned into deeds later.

Another factor to consider is the way the agreement will be sold to other parties whose interests have been represented by the negotiators, but who have not been personally present at the negotiation. Not everyone will appreciate a negotiator who gives up partisan advantage for the greater good. All parties may need to collaborate to sell the agreement they have made. It only takes one of them to try to get some extra credibility back home by portraying the result as a victory, to throw much of the positive work away. That is one of the reasons we are a bit lukewarm about the concept of win/win. In the context of developing healthier social capital, the real winner must be the organization! Is it therefore productive to portray individual outcomes from negotiations as wins? We think on balance the word is misleading.

Give plenty of time to agree a clear, common statement of what has been agreed or the state of progress, as appropriate. You may consider putting it in writing. This can be very useful in our complex world when memories are fallible at best, and even prone to a certain convenient selectivity from time to time. A typical agreement should be clearly worded and describe the deal in terms that are understandable to interested others who were not present at the negotiations. It should contain action details which are Specific, Measurable, Achievable, Realistic and Time-bound (SMART) and spell out who will do what, when they will do it and how often. Specifications about size, quality, reliability and other performance criteria should be explicit and precise with an indication of how achievement will be measured. Last there should be an agreed and effective contingency procedure for communicating when things start to go wrong or change dramatically or suddenly – as they almost always do.

Behaviour choices for market deal negotiations

The following list is offered as a reminder of the behaviours which make the market deals negotiating process an appropriate aid in the pursuit of enhanced performance and healthier social capital. They apply throughout all five stages and beyond.

- The aim is to build a working relationship which will sustain a high level of performance. Treat others with respect and demand the same courtesy. Listen to what they have to say and show clearly that you are listening to them by summarizing what you see and hear, both facts and feelings. By doing this you are showing them that you at least value their views, even if you do not always agree with them.
- Try to put yourself in other people's shoes.
- Ask for help in solving the problem. Asking for help in the right way increases each of the other participant's sense of self-worth and the likelihood of them offering some help or agreement.
- Negotiate as equals wherever possible. Even when the reality is that one or other has the power to issue an order, such a move is the resort of failure and destroys the deal.
- Be honest about what is relevant. This does *not* mean telling a few home truths about someone's abilities, personality or lineage! Perhaps authenticity is a more accurate description.
- Stick to your bottom line but do so politely. There are often other ways to help than giving up something you cannot afford to lose.
- Don't attack people. There are no productive responses to this in social capital terms.
- Offer help where you can. Your purpose is to resolve the conflict, get the best outcome and still have good working relationships in the future.

- Tackle any rising emotions or tension at the time by employing reflecting behaviours which show that you have noticed. By doing this you bring what could be a barrier to further progress, out into the open where it can be dealt with, instead of leaving it hiding in the shadows to create all sorts of inexplicable behaviours later.

Checklist

You may find this checklist helpful to assess the degree to which a market deals negotiating process or something like it already exists in your organization.

In my organization:

Negotiations are focused on getting the best outcome for the organization as a whole. | I Agree/I Disagree

Partisan victories are not valued. | I Agree/I Disagree

Negotiations reach a conclusion based on all parties having a clear understanding of each other's perspectives, problems and feelings. | I Agree/I Disagree

Negotiated solutions are owned by all the negotiating parties. | I Agree/I Disagree

When preparing to negotiate a deal, all parties analyse the subject and the relationships and plan how to work together to achieve the best results in both. | I Agree/I Disagree

When preparing, people spend enough time thinking about the working relationship and how to enhance it during the negotiations. | I Agree/I Disagree

During negotiations it is the common and accepted practice to communicate positive intentions. | I Agree/I Disagree

When negotiating, people are always honest about the difference between the outcomes they need and those they would like. | I Agree/I Disagree

When negotiating, everyone present follows the same set of known stages and has the same understanding of what each stage must achieve, so that the process is owned collectively. | I Agree/I Disagree

When negotiating, people refuse to make other people the problem. | I Agree/I Disagree

When people use the word win, they mean the organization as a whole. | I Agree/I Disagree

On reaching a solution, negotiating parties take time to ensure that the agreement is fully understood.	I Agree/I Disagree
When presenting the outcome to those who have not been present, there is never any question of partisan victory.	I Agree/I Disagree

If you either answered Disagree or perhaps wished there was a 'maybe' category, then some action on negotiating market deals would be helpful in the drive toward healthier social capital and better performance.

Confronting and conflict handling

Several times in this book we touch on the need to confront when it comes to developing healthier social capital. Confronting is a word which often carries more negative connotations than positive, and so perhaps we had better explain more fully why we are using such a provocative term.

As you will have discerned, an important aspect in both contracting and market deals is to confront the situation, not the person. When this is handled productively, it is possible to work together to find the best solution for the organization because people find it easier to sacrifice partisan advantage in favour of the greater good. If the confronting is handled badly, however, there will be little or no goodwill to allow real collaboration. So what is the difference between productive confrontation and destructive?

Productive confronting	Destructive confronting
Oriented toward future success	Oriented toward past failures
Describes behaviours and actions	Labels the person
Subject focused	Person focused
Uses clear and unequivocal language	Uses woolly and evasive language
Is open and honest	Feels like only so much of the agenda is visible
Respectful and courteous	Aggressive
Has a positive purpose which is declared up front	The purpose is unclear but there is an implicit intent to inflict damage
Aimed at building a relationship that will work in the future	Aimed at scoring points now

Invites candidness from the other person	Shuts the other person down
Comes with statements of positive intent for the outcome and the working relationship	Carries implicit messages of negativity

These can produce the following outcomes:

Both parties get clear about what is expected in terms of the quality of future interactions	Expectations are never spelled out and interaction standards are never made explicit
Both parties are clear about where actual performance falls short of expectations	Shortfalls in performance are only discussed in general terms or to score a point
Offers the chance to the other(s) to accept their shortcomings without losing face	Creates resistance in the other
Produces commitment to the achievement of agreed goals	Produces confusion and alienation and disables
Develops clear strategies for improving performance	Does not produce a clear way forward

Like contracting and market deals, confronting is based on the belief that every negotiator has two kinds of interests; those concerned with the subject matter of what they are trying to achieve and those concerned with securing high-quality interactions through a good working relationship with the other party in the future. The relative importance of these two goals varies depending on the circumstances and is very much a judgement for the individual to take at the time. There may be occasions when the subject goal is paramount. At other times it may be best to sacrifice some or all of the subject goal in order to buy a better working relationship for the future. This judgement will be reflected in the choice of behaviours adopted.

Healthy social capital is not about being nice for the sake of it, nor is it about winning at the expense of others in the organization. If the result is good for the whole organization in the short *and* the long term, then the choice was right. 'Social capitalists', as we might choose to call those who share our aim, have the discretion to choose what they believe to be the most productive and appropriate behaviours to fit each set of circumstances and the obligation to learn from the resultant experience.

If however we were to consider what the most common observable blend we would be likely to find in an environment of developing social capital, then it would be one which allocates equal importance to both the subject and the quality of future interactions. If there were a social capitalist's strategy of choice, this would be it.

You may have noticed that in all the talk of contracting and negotiating, there has been no word of compromise. For the reason, one has only to look at a dictionary definition, which describes compromise as 'a partial waiving of principles for the sake of settlement; neither one thing nor the other.' It doesn't stiffen the sinews much does it? It doesn't fire up the imagination and engage the spirit. It is the outcome that both parties feel they can live with or sell to their people back at the desk, boardroom table or assembly line. In fact in a negotiation involving parties who belong to the same community of interest, the same commonwealth, the same organization, this has to come a very poor second to the social capitalist strategy.

Checklist

You may find this checklist helpful to assess the degree to which productive confronting is already practised in your organization.

In my organization:

Confronting is seen as a positive thing. | I Agree/I Disagree

Productive confronting, as defined, is widely and skilfully practised. | I Agree/I Disagree

Confronting is subject and not person focused. | I Agree/I Disagree

Confronting is oriented toward future success and not past failure. | I Agree/I Disagree

Confronting is not aimed at scoring points over others. | I Agree/I Disagree

We don't play secret games when we need to confront an issue. | I Agree/I Disagree

People are prepared consciously to sacrifice a subject outcome for the sake of future working relationships if their judgement tells them that is the right thing to do. | I Agree/I Disagree

People choose and use the behaviours which reflect their judgement. | I Agree/I Disagree

People do not confront aggressively. | I Agree/I Disagree

Communicating respect is much more common than communicating blame. | I Agree/I Disagree

Confronting produces commitment to the achievement of agreed goals.	I Agree/I Disagree
Confronting produces the best outcomes for the organization as a whole and not just for the best negotiators.	I Agree/I Disagree
People do not set out to compromise.	I Agree/I Disagree

If you either answered Disagree or perhaps wished there was a 'maybe' category, then some action on confronting would be helpful in the drive toward healthier social capital and better performance.

Learning sets

Have you ever looked round the table at a meeting and wondered how much experience, knowledge and skill, how much real talent must be present – and how little of it is being used? At some gatherings there must be hundreds of years worth of this rich resource present.

One of the mediums we have used to liberate and utilize these riches in the pursuit of organizational success is learning sets which, as it happens, also provide an excellent forum for the development of healthy social capital: one which generates openness and trust in a setting where people from different functions who rarely meet otherwise, can get to know and respect one another. Learning sets, originally conceived and applied by Reg Revans (1983), represent both a living laboratory in which to practise the interpersonal skills and the process awareness required for a sense of community to take root, and a means to bring the wealth of experience and talent which can often lie dormant in organizations, to bear on live issues.

What follows is no more than a taster. There are a number of publications around which describe all the detail and nuances very well; for example, *Action Learning* by Ian McGill and Liz Beatty (1992).

Set membership

There are three roles in sets: the member, the presenter and the facilitator. There are up to six and not less than four set members, each of whom takes a turn at being presenter. Set membership is more or less permanent for the life of the set. There is only one facilitator and they are not a set member. They only visit as long as they are needed.

The roles explained

Presenter and *set member* are fully active roles throughout the duration of the set. Each set member has a responsibility to bring along a personal project, which must be a real and valued work issue. When a set meets, each set member has a half-hour time slot in which they present and have the full and undivided attention of the other members to help them move their project along. Sets should aim to meet every three weeks or so and the 'life' of any one set is usually around a year.

The *facilitator* does not bring a project to the set. Their primary role is to manage the process in the early stages so that members get full benefit.

The facilitator should aim to make their role redundant in time. Facilitator redundancy comes when the set has reached a state of maturity and no longer needs an external influence to keep it on track. Some sets can dispense with the facilitator early and some sets never really achieve it. For the set and its relationship with the facilitator, the journey to maturity is often described as starting from a hierarchical base, with the facilitator managing the process, then moving to a co-operative stage, with the facilitator gradually becoming less prominent, and finally reaching an autonomous state, when the facilitator is no longer required. Even then, the facilitator may be invited back to take a snapshot of the set at intervals to help them catch cosy ways of working as they try to creep in.

In addition to managing the process, facilitators must encourage the use of good behaviours within the set through appropriate interventions and by acting as a role model, particularly when the set first starts to meet. Facilitators require specialist training and some original talent.

How sets work

Successful sets are highly structured in terms of their processes and timings. With each presenter having a half-hour time slot to update their story from the last time and to prepare for the next step, a well run set meeting plays a bit like a series of unrelated, discrete but pacey agenda items. Time is used well and when a process is agreed, everyone sticks to it. The development of such disciplined time and process keeping is always a good indicator of the maturing set.

Members should come to each meeting ready to take their turn as presenter and to say how their project has progressed, what they have done, how it worked or didn't, what was unexpected, what learning was gained and what they plan to do next. When their own time slot comes around, it is often useful if the presenter starts by saying how they are feeling about the project. This may involve taking a personal risk like admitting to a mistake or showing some emotional vulnerability. When such confidences are respected over time then trust, that great lubricant in the affairs of organizations, begins to build.

As a rough guide on how much to say, the presenter should tell the story and not the *history*, confining themselves to the relevant factors affecting the immediate issue and always using the first person singular.

Once a set has begun to mature, presenters should also bring to the set some thoughts about *how* they want their time slot as presenter to run. Their selection of the most appropriate process option will depend on how their project is going. For example, if the presenter is feeling good about it, then they may welcome robust support. If on the other hand the presenter is feeling a bit insecure, they may welcome a more encouraging approach. If they have a clear way ahead, then they may simply want their set to test it to destruction before going live. If they are 'stuck', they may need the benefit of fresh perspectives.

Process options for presenters

The Reservoir Dogs tape

One of the most productive options is for the presenter to describe the part of their project that requires attention now and where they feel they need help. This should take no more than 3 minutes. The set members then have 3 more minutes to quiz the presenter for further information. Questions can be as probing as they like but must be for clarification only. Then the presenter is gagged. We have always treated this as a metaphorical description but if you have a strong Tarantino-esque bent and access to plentiful supplies of duck tape, then who are we to stand in your way. Don't blame us for any ensuing fatalities, however. Either way, the aim is to force the presenter to stay quiet, and, while they have nothing better to do, to listen while the set members discuss how they would tackle the issue from their own experience. At the same time, it prevents the presenter from closing down avenues of discussion prematurely with cold buckets of their reality. In the early days of a set's life, the facilitator will need to be quite firm with presenters who, in our experience, are prepared to try all sorts of non-verbal contortions to make their feelings known to their colleagues. The good news is that all the pain and suffering is worth it. Presenters are almost always pleasantly surprised by the breakthrough ideas that spring from these subject-naive discussions of their set.

Under the spotlight

Instead of gagging the presenter, the set members may interview him/her, asking them to explain their thinking by posing challenging and confronting questions. A variation on this theme is for one member to conduct the interview while the others observe and then debate what they have heard.

Collective creativity

Where there is, for instance, a problematic or even apparently insurmountable block to further progress, the presenter may ask the members to find a creative way forward.

Jump on the helicopter

The presenter can ask the members to provide a wider perspective on their issue by taking an overview of the context in which it is happening, sometimes called helicoptering.

The presenter must never relinquish ownership of their project or allow other set members to become involved beyond the confines of the set. If they do, the set will cease to exist and become instead, a project group. The power of the set lies in the ability of the members to keep the subjects presented at arm's-length. It is this detachment that provides the true value-add.

At the end of their time slot, presenters should say specifically what they are going to do before the next meeting. The other set members should challenge this for the SMARTness we touched on earlier.

Getting value from the investment in sets

To ensure that they are worthy of the investment, each set should reflect on its processes both at the end of each meeting and in a more structured way, at intervals of say five meetings. The criteria for a good return on investment are that there are specific, material, observable outcomes which the presenters and their managers can attribute to the work of the set, and that these have produced performance and behavioural improvements outside the set. In the wider context of the organization's social capital, the pay-offs come from new relationships, new networks and more three-dimensional people.

Checklist

You may find this checklist helpful to assess the degree to which the wealth of knowledge, talent and experience is already tapped in your organization.

In my organization:

We make full use of the wealth of knowledge, talent and experience we have at our disposal.	I Agree/I Disagree
Asking uninvolved others for help in thinking through problems, projects and ideas is already commonplace.	I Agree/I Disagree
Openness and trust are part of our normal currency.	I Agree/I Disagree
Naive questions are highly valued for the perspective they bring.	I Agree/I Disagree

People are already skilled in helping others get the best results.	I Agree/I Disagree
People are quite happy to discuss problems and failures with colleagues so that they can learn and get better results in the future.	I Agree/I Disagree

If you either answered Disagree or perhaps wished there was a 'maybe' category, then some action on introducing learning sets might be helpful in the drive toward healthier social capital and better performance.

Chapter 7

And now for something completely different

Through the unknown, we'll find the new
CHARLES BAUDELAIRE

Creativity and innovation have become buzzwords in today's business and management lexicon. Competitive advantage, greater flexibility, sustainable development – the arguments for why organizations need their people to be creative and innovative are already well rehearsed and documented elsewhere. Our main focus here is to explore the vital role that they can play in the creation of healthy social capital. Contrary to popular belief, organizational creativity and innovation are not the result of individual geniuses working in isolation, but are a collective enterprise. They are the products of people interacting and collaborating in shared ventures. Organizations that actively foster this interdependence and develop creative and innovative skills in their people at both an individual level and when they work together in groups can go a long way to meeting, not just their drive for self-interest, but their need to belong and to transcend that self-interest. This chapter offers a way forward to delivering these much sought after ingredients.

In practice, organizational creativity has enjoyed a rather chequered history. Until relatively recently, in many organizations it has been regarded with suspicion by all but the bravest and the status accorded to it somewhat ambiguous. Creative output has been seen as the preserve of particular functions such as R&D and Marketing, and, to some extent, as separate from real day-to-day business. In the remainder of the population, creativity has been at best something that is a valuable add-on and at worst, something to be discouraged for fear of mistakes. In general, it has not been regarded as an essential skill either for managers or for the organization as a whole.

The tide is turning, however. Continuous flux and transformation, both organizational and societal, is changing life almost unrecognizably. Within organizations, new skills and new ways of seeing and doing things are the order of the day. The initiatives of the 1980s such as Total Quality Management (TQM) and continuous improvement programmes, and the more recent radical and often brutal processes of Business Process Re-engineering that helped deliver greater effectiveness and efficiency have also had the effect of levelling the competitive playing field. Now they cannot alone deliver the paradigmatic shifts needed to enable organizations, not just to prosper, but simply to survive. To achieve these outcomes organizations need to do things differently in ways which resonate more with the needs of the people who work there.

Against this backdrop there is a growing recognition by Navigators and Flight Crew of the need for all their people to be able to think creatively and take creative action, but for many the gap between recognizing this and being able to make it happen still remains.

A whole range of factors can impact on an organization's ability to be creative and innovative, some structural, some cultural and some to do with the nature of contemporary work itself and later in this chapter we will be looking at these in detail and offering a way through them. As well as these, however, in our experience there is also something more fundamental operating, something that helps to account for that ambiguous position accorded to creativity.

In many organizations there seems to exist an underlying discomfort with and, at times, even a mistrust of the idea of 'creativity'. These feelings can manifest themselves differently depending on where in the organization you go. At Navigator and Flight Crew level creativity is often seen as not quite the serious stuff of business. It is not strategic enough, not systematic and logical, and its impact on bottom line results is difficult to evaluate. For the Core, epitomizing as creativity does, the moving on from the tried and tested and the quest for the new, it carries all the connotations of threat described in Chapter 5. Amongst the Activators and those who work for them, the reaction is very mixed. Some see it as something alien or downright terrifying while others would willingly embrace it if they were only given the encouragement and licence to do so. All these reactions are, for different reasons, not without some basis and result in a collective frame of mind that says 'we just don't do creativity here'.

This is borne out by the way in which the term 'creativity' itself is used. Within organizations, when talking about coming up with new ideas, new products and new ways of doing things, people frequently refer to it as 'being innovative'. While this owes much to the common confusion that surrounds the meaning of the words creativity and innovation (for definitions see pp. 171–2), we would suggest, however, that it also demonstrates the acceptability of the term 'innovation' over that of 'creativity'. The idea of innovation with its scientific, product and business connotation represents, for many people, a more comfortable, more acceptable option. Similarly, 'problem solving' with its focus on the practical and the analytical provides people with a safer, more accessible way of thinking about the creative process.

This underlying unease with the notion of personal creativity is wholly understandable and indeed we would be surprised if, to some extent, it was not in evidence. It reflects the much bigger picture – how creativity is viewed in society in general. Each of us has the ability to be creative, some would say it was hard-wired, and we already use it to some degree in our personal and professional lives. But, as a result of the process of socialization and education that most of us go through, we either don't recognize this or we doubt our ability. We are taught that creative people are 'special' individuals and that creativity is a rarefied activity to which most of us can never aspire. It is certainly not seen as something that the ordinary person in the street does as part of their normal day-to-day lives. Is it any wonder then that the very word creativity can cause fear, anxiety, or, in some cases, a helpless apathy when people are suddenly confronted with the dictum 'we need you to be creative'? It is an exceptional organization where an alternative portrayal of creativity prevails.

The mystique that surrounds creativity is further fuelled by the view that predominates in our society of the 'artist' as an eccentric genius who more often than not exhibits an unhealthy degree of individualism and egocentricity. This view misrepresents the creative process and has little relevance or usefulness in discussions of creativity in organizations. It leads to a focus on the creative process as an individual pursuit, the creation of a myth of the 'creative' personality and gives rise to the idea that, if you release a high level of creativity within people, the result could be chaos, even anarchy. In fact, the true profile of the creative person makes them candidates for the most wanted list in today's working environment and organizational creativity is such a group phenomenon that, if managed properly, it can foster interdependence and effective collective working.

Until these suspicions, fears and myths are addressed, creative action will continue to exist on the fringes of organizational life and the quest for the truly 'creative' organization will remain as elusive as ever. Instead of something which is integrated into the daily workings of the business, something that managers do naturally and willingly, creativity will be a somewhat hit or miss affair, limping along on an *ad hoc* basis unable to deliver consistently the results so desperately needed by today's and tomorrow's organizations. Most alarmingly, if left unchallenged, both creativity and innovation stand in danger of becoming yesterday's newspaper and of joining the ranks of the fads and the failed initiatives.

It is not surprising, then, that against this backdrop the idea of developing creativity within organizations has had such a mixed response, and unfortunately the types of programmes that many organizations have embarked upon have done little to assuage these feelings and beliefs. Whether arts based or focused only on creative thinking techniques, these have, in a number of ways, helped to reaffirm and even increase creativity's marginalization. The former tends to have limited business and strategic focus, with creativity often ending up as an end in itself rather than a means to an end. Similarly, creative thinking techniques, despite being powerful tools that have an essential part to play in the creative process, have a limited chance of becoming part of people's way of operating over time and of consistently delivering the results that organizations need. On their own they are not robust enough and without a mechanism to ensure that they are followed through and are given the support necessary for successful implementation, the ideas generated are very unlikely to be translated into reality. In these circumstances it is understandable that creativity is viewed as not sufficiently pragmatic and real world and remains on the fringes of organizational life rather than becoming embedded in day-to-day business. The message is clear. For creativity training to be effective and for it to have any credibility within the organization it must be both focused on what is real and important and be robust enough to become part of the way people work.

There does exist a compelling upside, however. For organizations that can find a way through the maze and successfully develop both creativity and innovation in their people, the rewards will be both substantial and gratifying. By tapping into and harnessing this latent power and energy, not only will they enjoy the improvement in current performance and bottom line results for which they are constantly striving, but they will be able to meet successfully those fundamental drives for self-interest and for integration that individuals pursue in their professional and personal lives, and, in so doing, create a more a satisfying workplace rich in social capital.

Before looking at the way forward we should briefly consider how developing organizational creativity and innovation can satisfy both the individual's need to act for self as well as their need to belong.

In Chapter 2 we saw how these two conflicting drives are ever present within humanity. On the one hand, as a species, human beings are autonomous, independent and self-reliant individuals acting in their own best interest. On the other, they also have a deep need to belong. They have a desire for integration into something bigger than, something outside of themselves, be it a family, a tribe, a community, a social group, an organization or a nation. The day-to-day lives of individuals represent a constant balancing act between the two, and, if one takes precedence over the other, it will, sooner or later, have a negative impact. If the need to belong becomes dominant, the result can be apathy and a lowest common denominator mentality. If, however, unfettered individualism and self-interest reign supreme, feelings of interdependence, empathy and identification are over-ridden and the organism can become a dangerous beast to itself and to those who have the misfortune to spend their working lives with it. In the pressure cooker existence of contemporary organizational life, there is little doubt that the latter has the upper hand and there is a pressing need to redress the balance.

Still, we have to be careful not to throw the baby out with the bath water. It is important to recognize the positive face of self-interest and individualism. Without this drive in some measure and the energy and focus that it produces, organizations and society would atrophy. They would not be dynamic organisms capable of adaptation, development and growth and would be unable to make those imaginative leaps that form the basis of social, cultural and scientific progress.

In order to be of benefit to the development of healthier social capital, creativity and innovation must work positively on both these conflicting drives. Their role in satisfying self-interest is, perhaps, the more widely accepted and travelled route, enhancing as they do the possibility of achieving personal goals, stretching and growing the individual's powers and giving them the self-confidence to tackle tasks they would not pre-viously have attempted. In the process they will feel engaged and exhila-rated. They will feel at once freer and more in control: and, if along the way, they are recognized and rewarded, that won't hurt either.

In essence, creativity and innovation can become highly absorbing, motivational and rewarding pursuits for an individual. They will be able to think for themselves and be more willing to take risks. They will be more likely to embark on individual initiatives of their own devising. So, rather than the 'loose cannon' image of popular myth, they will, in fact, possess skills and attributes highly appropriate to and much sought after in today's working environment.

It would be wrong, of course, to suggest that any process was one of unadulterated joy. Individuals who are empowered and engaged in the way described will also be liable to question, argue, debate and push relentlessly. There will be no sacred cows and, at times, this may make them uncom-fortable bedfellows: yet it is that abrasion, the spark and energy it produces, that is the very vehicle of change, progress and regeneration.

It is clear then that developing people's ability to be creative and innovative will take care of the drive for self-interest very nicely, but what about its adversary, the need for belonging and integration. In reality, in organizations there is a very strong collective flavour to the creative process. Beyond the initial formulation and articulation of a new idea by an individual, the interactions that give rise to that moment and support the idea's later development are much more of a collaborative effort than is commonly recognized. Creative ideas are not generated in a vacuum. They have their genesis in numerous conversations, discussions and pieces of information gathered and developed over time. Very rarely, if ever, are they the product of an individual working in isolation. Ideas can spring from formal collaborations where people are working together as a group exchanging information, experimenting and co-operating towards a shared goal or from the host of informal meetings, social interactions and chance encounters which are the stuff of organizational life.

Organizations that recognize this and encourage the existence of a network of opportunities for interaction and the exchange of ideas and provide training which develops both individual and group creativity will release and tap into this synergic energy and capitalize on its powerfully unifying force. Most importantly, they will also transform themselves into powerhouses capable of delivering sustained creativity and innovation.

Once an idea has been formed, its subsequent development as it moves through the organization and heads toward successful implementation is also almost exclusively a collective activity demanding a high degree of collaboration and effective co-operation. Planning the way ahead, steering its course and bringing the idea to fruition requires a range of complementary roles and skills not least of which are political acumen and organizational savvy. Acceptance and support for the idea must be successfully solicited. Words such as involvement, inclusion and unification are most appropriate here, and, by successfully winning the hearts and minds of people, initial feelings of individual achievement and satisfaction can be transformed into a shared collective experience.

So it is clear that collaboration and co-operation, in a variety of forms, are needed to feed and fuel these processes, and naturally, the quality of the interactions between people will play a major part in determining the relative success or failure of any venture. Organizations that focus on, develop and actively promote this interdependence and place the emphasis squarely on a shared goal, will reap the benefits that productive working relationships and empathy bestow on how people feel about the organization and their colleagues. In this way, developing both individual and collective creativity and innovation can become a powerful unifying force. Over time the sense of discovery, achievement and self-realization that creativity and innovative action provide come to be associated with a collective experience, strengthening the sense of community and reducing the current preoccupation with self. Creativity and innovation, if managed properly, are an excellent vehicle for building healthier social capital.

In the final analysis it comes down to the way in which creative energy is channelled. Developing people's ability to think creatively and take creative action, like everything else on today's organizational agenda, must be linked strategically to objectives and have current and future performance squarely in its sights. If creativity and innovation are to be the major assets they can be in the drive to deliver added value and competitive advantage, then organizations must ensure that the process they encourage is practical and results orientated. The rest of this chapter offers a tried and tested way to deliver just this.

The way forward

There currently exists both an opportunity and a challenge for organizations to seize the day and gain competitive advantage through sustained creativity and innovation. The way forward lies in successfully tapping into, nurturing and channelling the powerful creative drive present in all their people and building an environment sympathetic and conducive to creative thinking and innovative action taking. In addition, crucially, organizations must also acknowledge the existence of those two opposing drives, the pursuit of self-interest and the need to belong, and create the right mix in organizational life of individual self-realization and collective experience.

Creativity and innovation at work

How people in organizations approach the vital activities of creativity and innovation and the quality of the results they get is shaped in large part by the environment in which they operate. Where healthy social capital is present, people feel engaged and challenged. They feel more productive, more able to express themselves and less bound by artificial or self-imposed constraints. They generate ideas that are directly linked to the achievement of organization-wide goals. The following pages offer a guide to establishing a working environment within which people are willing and able to think creatively and take innovative action. But first, some definitions to set the scene:

The words 'creativity' and 'innovation' are often used synonymously but are, in fact, very different. Creativity has to do with generating new ideas while innovation is about introducing new ideas to the world and making them happen.

Our definition of creativity is:

Combining previously unconnected ideas, information and elements to make something new.

If this sounds too simple, and it has always seemed a bit more mystical and mysterious than that, then look around. Whether it relates to products, ways of working, systems or works of art, creativity involves combining thoughts and ideas to make new things. Look at any man-made object and you will find it is the result of a combination of other objects which someone has thought of putting together to make something new. This is important, because when we accept that combining is the essence of creativity, it becomes possible for us to believe we all can develop the skill.

Our definition of innovation is:

The process of turning new ideas into practical reality.

Innovation has to do with implementing ideas – wherever they come from. Being innovative in an organization can mean introducing any idea that changes or challenges the way things are done. It can be as straightforward as installing an already tried and tested system in a new department or as radical as bringing to fruition a completely new idea which has never been used before. Innovation is a practical process.

At every stage in the creative and innovative process there are opportunities for building and enhancing social capital through the involvement of others. People can work together to generate ideas, to plan for their implementation, and, as creative ideas turn to innovative action, there is tremendous scope for working across functional, departmental and hierarchical boundaries. As such, helping people to think creatively and to take innovative action can be a powerfully cohesive force and an instrument for winning hearts and minds.

New ideas go through a series of steps as they move from conception to fruition. This process is cyclical as Figure 7.1 shows. It is also fragile by nature and at any point these ideas can wither and die, or be killed off. If they are to survive they need help. Managers must nurture the practice, particularly in its early growth stage within the organization, encouraging the production of each new idea, and, once produced, helping it along to ensure the best chance of survival.

The way in which people experience their organization has a profound impact on the extent to which they will take creative and innovative action, or not. Crucial in the formation and maintenance of this experience are the ideas that exist and are shared within its boundaries and how these are translated into day-to-day behaviour. Its vision, values, knowledge and 'wisdom', and the assumptions it makes about itself and its operations, all play a major role in determining how people make sense of and interpret organizational life and consequently how they act. This shared awareness represents a vital driving force, giving people structure, direction and inspiration, as well as offering a rich body of knowledge and learned experience on which to base their actions. At the same time, however, it can also result in people seeing and interpreting issues and problems in too similar a way and taking similar types of action to deal with them. When this happens they tend towards the tried and tested, accepted ways of doing things rather than exploring new alternatives and new possibilities. The tricky role of

Figure 7.1. The cycle of organizational creativity and innovation.

extracting the best from the existing environment while, at the same time, encouraging the development of a new tradition rich in creative thinking and innovative action, falls, as always, to the leaders and managers.

Creativity, innovation and corporate goals

The organization's published goals, its vision and its plan, all broadcast the values it holds dear and, if creativity and innovation are to thrive, it is essential that they be given a prominent place there. Without this, it is very unlikely that many people will strike out on their own to find new ways of doing things. On the other hand, if Navigator and Flight Crew make a clear statement of intent and, if that is communicated throughout the organization, then the game is on for everyone to find ways in which they can join in. The same is true in formal performance reviews, which offer managers another opportunity to encourage and coach people to think differently and to generate new ideas. In so doing they make the process legitimate for the coachee and worthy of their investment of time and energy.

The physical environment

One very practical way in which managers can contribute to establishing a climate conducive to creativity and innovation is by creating a physical environment that encourages people to interact and exchange information and ideas. People who work in relative isolation, or who only ever come into contact with others doing the same type of work as themselves, are likely to think more narrowly about what they do and how they do it, than if they were able to share ideas and information readily and freely with people from other departments who see things from very different perspectives. It is this process of interaction and collective activity that acts as the stimulus for new ideas. Managers can help by creating spaces for chance meetings, spontaneous creative thinking sessions or just somewhere quiet to sit and think for a few moments. They can equip them with flip charts or whiteboards so that thoughts and ideas can be explored more easily, even reading material unrelated to work to stimulate thought processes.

Positive behaviours

Positive sentiments like enthusiasm, optimism and confidence must be encouraged. Even passion has a place! People who are passionate about what they are doing tend to create more and constantly strive for their cause. A friend recently referred to someone he had met as a 'radiator' and when asked what he meant, he explained that he saw two kinds of people; radiators and drains. Radiators, he said, give out warmth and enthusiasm with their positive, 'can do' attitude while drains just suck the energy out of me with their black, negative, 'it will never work approach.' In that case, managers at all levels must be model radiators for their people.

Another, slightly alien thought, is for managers to encourage people to think differently by introducing a measure of playfulness at work. Humour, for example, relieves stress, helps mental flexibility and makes work a more enjoyable experience all round. In so doing, it offers a resonance with the whole person, rather than just the bit that has to get the work done. It lightens the mood, but it does not have to cut across the imperatives of goals and deadlines to do it. In fact, by enhancing the work experience, it makes a successful conclusion more likely and certainly can be instrumental in encouraging the frame of mind, both individual and collective, that makes creativity and innovation much more likely.

Looking up and out

Creativity and innovation depend on people broadening their horizons; looking up and out and focusing on the future rather than the past. By collecting information from as wide an area as possible, from internal and external customers, from competitors, from organizations in the same and in different fields of operation; by keeping track of the latest thinking and encouraging others to do the same, managers send a strong message about challenging 'the way we do things' and seeking out new opportunities.

Risk-taking

In establishing an internal climate that encourages and facilitates creativity and innovation, managers must look at and question their *own* attitudes and behaviours as well as those of others. Risk-taking for example, is an area which often stimulates heated debate. While few would argue that taking risks is anything other than essential to their survival and success, most organizations we have encountered could, in practice, be described as rather risk averse. It is certainly self-evident that risk, creativity and innovation go hand in hand. However the alternative, 'business as usual,' is just as risky. After all, if you do what you've always done, there is a very good chance that you will get the results you've always had. In an atmosphere where nothing changes, nothing new is produced. Few organizations now find themselves in this kind of static environment. As a result, it is imperative that managers actively encourage calculated risk-taking. Naturally they will want to ensure that the risks are well planned and resourced and thereby minimized. They can then use any 'intelligent failures' that result, as opportunities to encourage people to reflect, learn and feel better about their ability and new scope they have for future creative and innovative actions.

Capability, opportunity and motivation

For people to take creative action they have to want to. Whether or not they want to will depend on how capable they perceive themselves to be, the scope and opportunity they feel they have, how they think their actions will be received and the extent to which they believe they will benefit personally. Along with creating positive versions of the rest of these conditions, managers must therefore also ensure that everyone possesses the necessary skills.

Thinking creatively is an ability everyone has. We are born with it. Look at children when they play. They are excited and uninhibited, using their imagination to change everyday objects into whatever they want them to be. Armchairs become sailing boats, a pile of bricks becomes a castle. As we get older, this uninhibited enjoyment of creativity becomes tempered by social values, personal inhibitions, lack of confidence, the need to conform and so on, with the result that most of us use only a fraction of our creative potential. We still have this ability, however, and we can develop it and become skilled in using it (see the Uccello™ Process on p.178).

In order to stimulate that development, foster the necessary skills and make the organization a place where generating and implementing creative ideas is the norm, the following training may be needed:

- using the Uccello™ Process;
- goal setting for creativity;

- managing and facilitating ideas meetings;
- making presentations;
- problem solving;
- coaching skills;
- influencing;
- strategic planning.

In addition, managers will also need to give people more freedom to think actively about their work and more responsibility for finding innovative ways of achieving agreed goals. Talking about creativity and innovation is easy, and even putting systems in place which encourage them isn't all that difficult, but finding the time and the courage to actually do things differently is another matter entirely. Exploring the possibilities takes time, and if people are not accorded sufficient, they will simply seek out the shortest route to a solution. This might not sound too bad at first, but the shortest route is often also the most familiar. The likely outcome? Same old, same old ... One barrier to progress in this respect occurs when the drive for current output is so dominant that managers feel unable to give their people the time and space to explore other possibilities. As a consequence they deny themselves and the organization the potential for better products, processes and ways of working in the future. To overcome this, managers must have the courage to be explicit, communicating their expectations about creativity and innovation clearly and backing them up with tangible action. As always, words must be backed by consistent action if they are to be believable. The commitment need not be huge; simply building in time for generating ideas when planning a project time-line can be enough. The encouragement of small, self-managed work groups, like the learning sets discussed in Chapter 6, can also be helpful as they allow people a safe place to practise working in a more 'entrepreneurial' manner. By giving people greater freedom, responsibility and opportunity to think and act creatively, such measures tell them both how much they are valued and what is expected of them.

Being creative can be highly motivating. People enjoy producing new ideas and really, all managers have to do to encourage it, is make it possible. However, it is important to sound a cautionary note, because, when it comes to creativity, it is well established that the more traditional methods of motivating through the use of targets and rewards are not particularly effective. In fact, they are quite likely to achieve the opposite of what was intended. In her article *How to Kill Creativity*, Theresa Amabile (1999) makes it clear that people produce less numerous, and poorer quality ideas, when pressure is applied and creative thinking is demanded 'to order.' What works instead is to create an environment where people *want* to generate ideas. By giving them stretching but achievable challenges in their work and by assigning tasks that allow them to use their creative skills, managers can send a clear, motivating message that will encourage individuals and groups of people to work together in the vital pursuit of creativity and innovation. When they use the Uccello® Process with others, there is a sense of excitement and challenge as they push for more and more, new, and potentially unique ideas. There is camaraderie as they work together and a huge sense of achievement when they produce a new idea that they know will meet their purpose. In fact the communal nature of the experience can be a major motivator in itself, which not only gives rise to performance enhancing ideas but also serves to make a significant contribution to the development of healthier social capital.

Involving others and gaining acceptance for new ideas

In order for new ideas to become a reality, the originator(s) almost invariably find(s) they must involve people outside the immediate group. These might be Flight Crew whose support and backing is needed, but may also be any peers and colleagues who can either add value or who have an interest. New ideas are fragile, however, so the originators of the idea must plan and choose their first external contact with care. A friendly and positive ear can be highly energizing while a negative response of the 'we tried that before and it didn't work then' variety can prove to be the kiss of death, not only for this idea but for the motivation to try again. It doesn't tend to do the health of social capital much good either.

If it is ultimately to succeed, a new idea usually has to be able to survive beyond the originating group and whatever first contact allies they have been able to secure. For it to float, an idea's first outing into the wider organization must be as well planned and managed as the launch of a ship. All the usual problems encountered by those responsible for introducing change apply, in fact even more so. There is something intrinsically threatening about creativity and innovation that sparks off many of the resistance behaviours and feelings discussed in Chapter 4. These must be addressed with patience and determination until people come to terms with the fact that seeking out new and different ways of working, as well as finding new products and markets, needs to become a way of life in the twenty first century. If these people cannot be brought on board, serious consideration should be given to hoisting them over the side of the ship at the earliest opportunity.

The identification and enlistment of allies who will ease the passage of a new idea, particularly in the earliest stages, is therefore vitally important. A credible and influential champion will be essential if opposition on any scale is anticipated. Different people in the organization will have a stake in making a new idea succeed or fail and each will have his or her own criteria against which the idea will be judged. To give it the best chance of success therefore, an idea must be presented to the decision makers in ways that are relevant to them. Aligning the idea with organizational or departmental objectives and demonstrating the value-add that will accrue is one obvious strategy.

Endorsement by the decision makers clears the way for the new idea to be introduced to those who will implement it. Winning their hearts and minds is a priority. If they buy-in and commit themselves to making it a reality, they become disciples not only of the idea itself, but also of the importance of creativity and innovation for the future well-being of the organization.

With enough people working in creative and innovative ways, a critical mass can be achieved and then such behaviour becomes the norm. However, in order to sustain the practice in the face of the usual other pressures, it can be worthwhile to consider creating a regular forum for the specific purpose of talking about new ideas and how they can be developed. This gives creativity and innovation the place they deserve and avoids the ever-present danger of the topic being relegated to a late item at the monthly meeting which, when time runs out, is shelved. Consistent with the topic, the forum should be conducted in a non-threatening, light way so that people can express themselves freely and with humour. Creativity and innovation should also feature regularly in any briefing process the organization has in operation. Whatever form the communication process takes it must keep creativity and innovation in the public eye.

Sessions about creativity require a particular style of managing in order to get the best from them. For example, some guidelines agreed with the group for how they will behave towards each other will help, as will a light hand on the tiller to allow people the freedom to express themselves while still staying on course. Since creativity does well from the coming together of different approaches and ways of thinking, a kind of 'creative abrasion' should be cultivated along with a diversity of membership. A tip for these kind of meetings is to invite an 'alien': someone from outside of the immediate circle who has an interest in what is going on but has little or no relevant expertise. 'Aliens' have the advantage of being able to ask naive questions without feeling foolish. They can challenge the group's thinking and offer insights that might not otherwise be available. Facilitators with the tools to work with creative groups can also be useful.

People interact and collaborate at every stage in the process of generating and implementing new ideas. Incorporating creativity and innovation into the organization's normal ways of working will therefore be of material help in the journey towards better performance and healthier social capital.

The Uccello™ Process

This chapter so far has been about fostering a climate that encourages creativity and innovation and the role of managers in making this a reality. Now we will look at the Uccello® Process which individuals and groups of people working together can use to develop creativity and innovation, and, to generate those winning ideas that will help deliver improved performance, and, where appropriate, competitive advantage.

We have run workshops using this process for many types of organization ranging from public relations to construction and finance, and, by working with people to develop their skills in this area, have helped them produce countless new and original ideas, many of which have been implemented and are still contributing to the bottom line results in their organizations. (For a more detailed guide to using the Uccello® Process see *Non Stop Creativity and Innovation* by Fiona McLeod and Richard Thomson, published by McGraw-Hill, 2001). Figure 7.2 shows what the Process looks like.

It comprises eight steps, the first six of which relate to creativity, and the last two to innovation. The first step naturally is to identify the subject. Getting this clear sets up a useful tension between what is wanted and what currently exists. Workshop participants are asked to consciously focus their attention on the future in order to open up their minds and find real alternatives and potentially dramatically different ways of doing things rather than simply adapting and amending what they already have. Tutors encourage groups to spend time exploring their purpose and thinking very carefully about it. As they do so, the definition changes and becomes subtler. For example, one group started with a stated desire to find

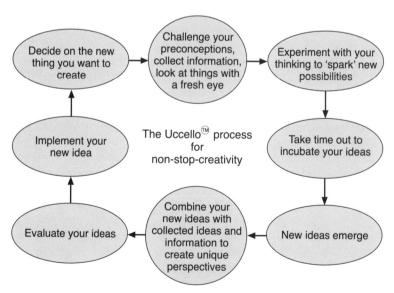

Figure 7.2. The Uccello® Process.

a new way of advertising what they had to offer. After a short time this became 'a new way to let the world hear our voice', a subtlety which allowed them to find a radically different solution to the problem.

In the second step the ground is prepared for new ideas. Mindsets and preconceptions are challenged. Things are looked at from different perspectives and minds opened to new possibilities. It has been found, not surprisingly, that people who consistently come up with new ideas tend to be eclectic collectors of information. They do not limit themselves to reading about their own industry or occupation, but are interested and curious about everything, avidly seeking out information from as many sources as possible. They are flexible in their thinking and their open-minded attitude helps them to spot opportunities that no one else has seen. Because they are working with a rich bank of material, they are able to generate more imaginative and more original ideas. In the workshops therefore we encourage participants to set about collecting information and ideas from a wide range of diverse sources to provide the building blocks for their work.

In our day-to-day lives we all have shorthand ways of thinking about and doing things. These are built up from past experience and are indispensable. They enable us to process information, make decisions quickly and multi-task. They help us function with reasonable efficiency in a complex world. The difficulty, however, is that when our thinking is automatic in this way it closes down our ability to be creative. To help free up our thinking and to generate new ideas, we need something to act as a trigger to help us breakout of the confines of these 'set' patterns. In step three of the Process participants consciously experiment with their thinking by applying some tools and techniques to the chosen purpose that will act as triggers and spark off new creative possibilities. They might think about the opposite of it, or they can choose to redefine it so that they can look at it from a different standpoint. They might also develop a metaphor for it which can help with its exploration and remove preconceptions. Experimenting with thinking in this way helps people to 'think out of the box'.

In the next step of the Process the unconscious is brought into play. Having defined the purpose, challenged preconceptions and experimented with thinking, it is time to relax. Slowing our mind down by doing something different or simply resting, allows the unconscious to make new and interesting combinations. It will connect ideas and information in ways we would not have done while fully alert.

And so, in step 6, we come to the essence of creativity – combining. Combining the ideas that have been generated while working through the Process with other ideas and information gathered, makes for unexpected and unusual results. To create something new in a business context it is usually necessary to look beyond the immediate sphere and to the future. In this step workshop participants are asked to take any of their ideas and combine them with anything new that is happening in:

- their immediate work team;
- their organization;
- their industry;
- other industries;
- the world in general;
- or with 'blue sky ideas': that is to say, anything that interests them – music, theatre, golf, current affairs, whatever.

Combining always results in some highly original and competitive edge ideas. Also, because they are related directly to a defined purpose, they are relevant and have a practical focus.

This marks the end of the ideas generating steps in the Process. The final two steps are about innovation.

We have found that when groups are using the Uccello™ Process, they initially appear quite inhibited and produce a relatively small number of ideas. They hold back, weighing up each one before saying it aloud for fear of sounding foolish. This reticence disappears, however, as soon as they come to accept that they should not judge their ideas too early and that they will have the opportunity to evaluate them all once the creative process is over. Having relaxed into the process, they then go on to make very imaginative connections and combinations and produce a large number of radical ideas.

These must now be evaluated and a selection made of the ones to be progressed. To evaluate ideas people can use any decision-making tool although we prefer to use a specifically designed decision grid. This involves selecting five ideas from those generated and scoring each against a series of headings including:

- Will it meet our purpose?
- Is it new to our team or our organization?
- Will it contribute to achieving corporate goals?
- Will it add value for the customer?
- Can we produce it at low cost?
- Is it high risk?
- Do we like it?

Each heading is then weighted according to its relative importance and the potential value to the organization and is scored. This is not intended to show definitively the best idea. Rather, it helps in prioritizing. It organizes the thoughts and reduces the options to a manageable number.

Finally, a plan must be made to implement the selected idea. This must include an assessment of the key players whose buy-in will be needed to ensure that the idea has a fighting chance of success.

The Uccello™ Process takes people on an eight step journey from identifying the focus of attention all the way to implementation. It can be carried out by one individual but more usually involves others. When managers work to create a climate within which creativity and innovation are the norm, where new ideas are welcomed and helped to become a reality, people will feel good about themselves, they will enjoy working in an organization that values them and they will give more of themselves. The pay-offs for organizations will be improved performance, better bottom line results and healthier social capital.

Checklist

You might find this checklist useful in determining whether your people are ready to be creative and your organization prepared for innovation.

In my organization:

People are encouraged to do things differently and not simply follow the 'tried and tested' route. I Agree/I Disagree

People are regularly given projects and assignments that are interesting, challenging and have scope for creative thinking. I Agree/I Disagree

Our work environment is structured to allow people who do not normally work together to interact. I Agree/I Disagree

Change is welcomed as a positive force. I Agree/I Disagree

Calculated risk-taking and 'risky thinking' are promoted and supported. I Agree/I Disagree

Failure which results, not from stupid mistakes, but from honest and well resourced attempts, is viewed as a learning opportunity. I Agree/I Disagree

Situations and problems which are ambiguous and ill-defined are promoted as opportunities for creative thinking. I Agree/I Disagree

Creativity and innovation are talked about throughout the organization. I Agree/I Disagree

In the work environment it is accepted that fun and professionalism are good for business. I Agree/I Disagree

There is an atmosphere of optimism and confidence where people are positive and negativity is discouraged. I Agree/I Disagree

Measurable goals for increasing creativity and innovation are set in all areas of the organization. I Agree/I Disagree

Forums exist for new ideas to be presented and built upon prior to presenting them to a wider audience.	I Agree/I Disagree
People feel equipped and able to make decisions that affect how they work and their ability to achieve targets.	I Agree/I Disagree
People have been trained in creative thinking and ideas generating techniques.	I Agree/I Disagree
Collaborative working between groups, departments, divisions etc. is encouraged.	I Agree/I Disagree
We employ reward systems designed specifically to encourage creativity and innovation.	I Agree/I Disagree
Our style of working enables people to be 'entrepreneurial' in how they operate.	I Agree/I Disagree
Time is set aside in meetings or we have meetings specifically for generating new ways of doing things.	I Agree/I Disagree
Our business structure allows people to work in small autonomous work groups.	I Agree/I Disagree
People are skilled in managing conflicting opinions to achieve a common goal.	I Agree/I Disagree
People know how to influence those who can help progress creative ideas.	I Agree/I Disagree
We hold regular reviews of how new ideas have been introduced.	I Agree/I Disagree
In ideas generating sessions we involve people from outside our discipline to introduce a fresh or unusual perspective.	I Agree/I Disagree
We support each other when new ideas are rejected.	I Agree/I Disagree
People are trained in communicating, making presentations and influencing in order to help them introduce new ideas into the organization.	I Agree/I Disagree
Systems and procedures exist for promoting and fast-tracking new ideas.	I Agree/I Disagree
A tradition exists of leaders championing and promoting new ideas and projects.	I Agree/I Disagree
The criteria for evaluating and judging ideas have been agreed and disseminated throughout the organization.	I Agree/I Disagree

Opportunities exist for people to meet and network with key decision makers and opinion formers.	I Agree/I Disagree
People are skilled in planning strategically to implement their new ideas and are supported during the process.	I Agree/I Disagree
Funds exist specifically for the introduction of new ideas.	I Agree/I Disagree
Supporting and helping in the implementation of new ideas is valued and recognized.	I Agree/I Disagree

If you either answered Disagree or perhaps wished there was a 'maybe' category, then you might consider developing your people's creativity and innovation skills and so gain the benefits in performance, motivation and healthier social capital.

Chapter 8

A glance down some other interesting avenues and a pocket summary

Willing hands and the freedom to fulfil destinies are what create strong economies
WALL STREET JOURNAL

What a depressingly stupid machine!
MARVIN THE ROBOT, IN DOUGLAS ADAMS'
LIFE, THE UNIVERSE AND EVERYTHING

As work becomes more complex and collaborative, companies where people work together best have a competitive edge
DANIEL GOLEMAN IN
WORKING WITH EMOTIONAL INTELLIGENCE

Throughout this book we have concentrated pretty well exclusively on behaviours, processes and ways of working, and, for those who like to start books at the end or just want a brief overview, that content is summarized in the last part of this brief chapter. However, these are not the only conditions which organizations can employ to advantage. If we have appeared to play down the importance of the non-behaviourial factors in organizations' quest for success, such was not our intention, but rather because that is not where our experience lies.

With their interdependencies and chains of cause and effect, organizations possess a machine-like quality. If you listen closely enough you can almost hear it sometimes. You can certainly tell the difference very quickly between one that is running well and one that is not, even if you can't immediately put your finger on the reason. Like all machines, it is important to keep each of the component parts in good condition and properly tuned to deliver whatever the particular machine was built to do. Making the right choices about what to change and what to leave well alone, drawing the distinction between unnecessary fiddling and essential tuning is critical. Here are some things that are happening in the non-behavioural area which, properly handled, can be a real asset in the pursuit of healthier social capital. It follows of course that, handled badly, or at the wrong time, or as the sole panacea, they have the capacity to be a bit of a disaster as well.

Some other interesting avenues

The physical bricks and mortar, steel and plastic

Workplace design has been around for a long time but that in no way diminishes the contribution it has to make to the development of healthy social capital. For one thing, the chances of people meeting to contract for better Key Interactions, or negotiate market deals, work in learning sets and Planning Groups, or generate creative ideas together will be greatly enhanced if the physical conditions are inviting. For another, the social contacts, those casual encounters unrelated to any given piece of work which are so important to any community, can only happen if the physical structure of the workplace allows them.

Traditional building design has, in the past, given rise to circumstances where, for instance, people on one floor of the same building barely even recognize colleagues from another. These were not conditions sympathetic to a developing sense of community, but that is changing. Exciting innovations, highly compatible with the development of social capital, are already taking place. Forward thinking organizations are building environments which are friendly to both work and social needs – dugouts and action zones for impromptu meetings, for example – breakout structures with wall-sized whiteboards, great for project groups and learning sets.

To address the need for casual contact and the serendipitous sharing of ideas and information, some organizations are taking steps to identify where people like to gather and then placing things like coffee machines and water dispensers there to encourage more of it. This is definitely the best way round to do it. Have you ever seen a local park where the official paths are all neatly laid out, but the real paths are immediately obvious in the worn tracks cutting across the grass? That is the same principle at work. Relatively inexpensive too and a real pointer to people about how you want them to go about their business.

Others have taken to putting up glass walls instead of plasterboard. This may seem a bit of a gimmick but people like the implicit message of honesty, transparency, and nothing to hide. Indeed, there is quite a long history of enlisting the physical environment to help change behaviour. Was it really way back in the 1970s when in *Up the Organisation*, Robert Townsend suggested nailing up the Chief Exec's door to force him to go walkabout and meet his people?

These kind of signals are not lost on people. They speak volumes about the way the organization would like people to work together. They act as open invitations to collaborate in knowledge exchange and sharing of ideas. Like many signals they may need to be interpreted and amplified and reinforced before people will really understand them and believe the message: but that is true of each of the ingredients of healthy social capital.

The corporate village – a sinister development or natural progression?

People are using the term, corporate village, to describe a range of developments all of which have a contribution to make to the development of healthy social capital. Crèches, including the granny variety, on-site chefs and company bars, visiting masseurs and psychotherapists to help reduce stress, fitness centres, nap areas, on-site jogging trails, and 'bring your pets to work' policies are just some of the creative means organizations are using now to attract and retain the best staff in competitive labour markets. Some larger organizations have invested in on-site restaurants, banks and shops, and there seems to be increasing evidence that the investment is a sound one.

To service these new environments, other industries are springing up. Some employees even have access to their own lifestyle manager who will basically do the things you don't have time for in your busy working life, like shopping, having the car serviced and so on. OK, so some managers will reckon they always had that anyway in the shape of secretaries and personal assistants (although these people themselves may not agree), but this new development seems to be less restricted to the higher echelons and have more to do with attracting and retaining excellent performers wherever they sit in the organization.

Some see these innovations as a cynical move to encourage long hours and presenteeism, to make it more attractive for people to stay at work than go home, and it is easy to see why a misguided employer might indeed view this as an opportunity to be seized and exploited. Societal trends are working in their favour, after all. With more and more people living alone, the friendly office where all the comforts are provided may well seem more attractive than a solitary flat, loft or even mansion, where the vacuuming and the washing are the primary sources of excitement.

But is that a good enough argument to condemn the whole idea of corporate villages? After all, any new development in the history of humankind has tended to have both positive and negative potential and usually someone who is prepared to exploit the latter. If, on the other hand, we start with the premise that the Navigator of an organization wants to develop healthier social capital in their organization, will they not be more likely to shun and even take steps to guard against the negative potential? Will they not see that a long hours culture is destructive of the very thing that they are trying to create?

Even the friendliest corporate family is likely to be as suffocating and inhibiting as real families can sometimes be if they are the *sole* source of belonging. Furthermore, people are not daft. If the organization sets out to exploit them, it isn't usually too long before they notice, and eventually the exploited will kick back. When they notice, the best ones move on, defeating the whole purpose of the exercise, which, as you will recall, was to attract and retain the best people so that they could deliver the best results. Even if they don't move on, the alternative could be worse for the exploiter. They may stay! And it is surprising how quickly a long hours, presenteeist culture can take the shine off the most creative and sparkling of performers. Not all of them, of course! A few may thrive, but most people need something more in the way of balance in their lives, both inside and outside of work, and will ultimately come to resent even the most lavish of prisons. So, as always, exploitation is a short-term strategy at best and has nothing to do with healthy social capital.

Indeed, a number of astute and forward-looking organizations are already clearly aware of the diseconomies of long hours cultures and are taking steps to discourage the practice. That this is not entirely driven out of altruism or social conscience should not be a source of either surprise or criticism. Organizations work better with people to help them, whose lives are well rounded and balanced, and people work better in organizations which allow them to be so. And that fact should be a source of comfort to those of us who harbour some lingering fears of a future which embodies the worst exploitative excesses of a corporate village environment. A life centred entirely around work, and circles of friends composed entirely of colleagues, carries dangers of loss of perspective and cosy thinking reinforced by like minds – both are the hallmarks of a closed community. Communities that are closed to outside influences and developments are at serious risk.

Organizations are therefore right to be careful, but there is little doubt that the corporate village has many positives to offer. A sense of community helps people identify with a common cause, with a commonwealth in which success and future well-being depend on the effectiveness of collective inter- actions and interdependencies – all very consistent with healthy social capital. There are a lot of good ideas on the subject out there, for anyone who cares to look.

Restructuring – a good investment?

There is a curious tendency apparent amongst organizations faced with the need to respond to a change or a crisis or an opportunity – they restructure. For many it seems almost to be the weapon of choice for all occasions. The reason for this is puzzling. In fact, in our experience, we cannot recall a situation where the structure was the main culprit. Sometimes structures help a bit and sometimes they get in the way a bit, but even then, people can usually find a way round them if they really want to. And what makes the popularity of restructuring even more surprising is the cost. This is not a cheap option. Never mind the direct costs which can be substantial. There is the disruption, the new relationships, the break-up of old ones, the distrac- tion of individual and group attention from real and vital tasks and the dilution of skills, to name just a few of the downsides. And lastly, there is the most fundamental objection of all. What do you have at the end of it? Have you solved the problem? Are you better equipped to deal effectively with your crisis or your opportunity? Our view is that this will only be so if you have got down to the roots of the problem. Otherwise you will just have bought yourself another vehicle to fail in. Rather than getting involved in such an expensive and potentially wasteful venture, we suggest that organ- izations ask themselves the question, 'Was it the structure wot done it?' and if the answer is anything but a resounding 'Yes', they should look around for a more worthwhile cause to invest in.

It is true of course, that structures, systems and procedures must be addressed. Not many organizations can run without them, but they are not the primary drivers of excellent performance. They are enablers. As such, they should *not necessarily* be the first thing an organization tackles when facing major change. So, if your natural inclination is to lead with restruc- turing as your opening gambit for developing healthier social capital, please try to resist the temptation. You can always do it later when the ground is more fertile.

E-mails, the Web and all that

Communications technology like e-mail, videoconferencing, intranet and the Web are now central to the working practices of many organizations. The speed and scale of this development gives it a bit of a wild west and covered wagon feel. Everything is new and evolving. Will it prove to be a great boon or a Frankenstein monster? Will the increased quantity and accessibility of information mean better quality or just more? Even as we write some companies are reportedly starting to re-examine the economics of e-mail. And what of the workers? Will there be consequences for face-to-face contact and what might that mean for social capital? It is certainly an issue worthy of some close attention.

On the one hand, the power and speed of these communications media, along with their ability to capture, manipulate and exchange knowledge, information and experiences, undoubtedly offer organizations the prospect of competing more successfully, and even broadening the scope of their horizons to encompass the whole globe should they wish. There is also much current talk about the pros and cons, not to say the feasibility and desirability, of virtual communities. There is certainly need for caution. Few innovations are universally beneficial and there is the constant danger that the many advantages blind its practitioners to the potential threats. Ultimately, technology is a tool, a means to an end. As for all organizational systems and processes, it must serve the people and not the other way round. Getting this bit right may be one of the neat tricks of the decade.

Terms and conditions

This is more familiar territory for organizations wishing to attract and retain the best people and encourage them to produce their best work, but even here the thinking is changing.

Financial reward will always be a favourite of course but it has long been recognized as a blunt instrument when used in isolation. Mercenaries are, after all, not really required to be loyal to anything but the current highest bidder. What is needed is a set of benefits and perks which attract and retain the right kind of people at the same time as they support the development of healthier social capital. Cafeteria-style benefits packages, which allow people at different stages in their lives to select the rewards that best suit them at the time, fit these criteria rather well for example. They give out a message that the organization is concerned with the whole person and not just that bit with the valuable skills. On-line shopping breaks, regular sabbaticals, and the crèches we mentioned on p. 187, say similar things.

A pocket summary

In part, this book has been about creating the conditions which allow people to feel good about themselves, each other and the organization in which they spend much of their waking lives – but only in part. This is not a do-gooders bible. This is about bottom line performance, about unleashing the potential of the human resource on the goals of the organization and producing sustained, and constantly self-improving, excellent performance.

Organizations have the chance to release that potential, particularly now when society is increasingly failing people's basic need to belong. People can make the difference, but they recognize a poor deal when they see one, and that is what in many instances, they are currently being offered. They get to work harder and longer with less security and with people they know less and less well. They are exhorted to loyalty and to work as a team but are recognized and rewarded individually, and only for so long as it suits the organization they work for. It is little wonder that they respond by accepting the deal and looking after themselves.

And yet while this is happening there is a door sitting ajar just waiting to be pushed open. Our hereditary drive for self-interest is already well catered for, but not so our need to belong, to feel part of something important. There is a gap in the market for those organizations willing to make the necessary investment to fill it. In return for this investment they can expect to attract the best people, retain them, and, by winning their hearts and minds, encourage them to contribute all they are capable of to the common wealth of the organization.

They won't be easy to manage, mind you. They will have ideas and will take some convincing when their schemes don't fit with the overall direction of the organization or have a lower priority than others. Your managers will need new skills and will have to come to believe in the importance and status of their new roles. They will have to focus their attention more on influence than control, process than task, and strategic thinking than operational detail.

But get the people right and you can even get away with some poor systems, inappropriate structures and ageing technology, for a time at any rate. Of course it is not necessary that you put up with such things because the fully engaged workforce will help you create the systems that fit well with your needs, build a structure which facilitates business rather than impeding it, identify the most appropriate technology and whatever else you need. The beauty of this approach, is that the people of the organization will see what they have constructed and know it is theirs. They will be rich in healthy social capital and they will not allow such a joint venture to do anything else but excel.

First and foremost, performance is about people, the way they behave, the way they perceive each other, the extent of their true engagement with individual, unit and organization-wide goals and the quality of their interactions with key others inside and outside the organization. People will bring all sorts of qualities to the party if they are allowed. They will bring sound judgement and common sense to temper flights of fancy. They will bring courage, stamina and determination to deliver what they believe in, commitment and enthusiasm and hitherto unsuspected creativity. The potential pay-off for enlisting these talents and energies is huge. What on earth would life be like if most of the workforce started to behave in ways which would hitherto have been considered exceptional?

Chapter 9

A tactical guide to investing in social capital

The return for investing in social capital is a workforce who feel a sense of connection to the objectives of the organization as a whole and who are prepared to give more of themselves to see those objectives achieved than they otherwise would, and on more occasions than they thought they were capable of. What they get in return is the fulfilment of both their self-interest need and their need to belong to a community – what we describe as healthy social capital. While there are other conditions which can help bring about healthy social capital, we have concentrated on the area we have worked in for the last 15 plus years, and which we also believe has the greatest contribution to make in this context, namely behaviours, processes and ways of working. It is probable that many organizations will have a number of these or something very like them already in place. However there may be gaps, and so we have provided this short guide to help you consider how best any action might be positioned to achieve maximum positive impact on both the social capital of your organization and its ability to consistently produce excellent bottom line results.

If you have reached this page via the rest of the book then you will note that we have reverted to the more generic titles of leader for chief executives and the like, senior manager, middle manager and first line/ opinion formers. This is purposely to accommodate those readers who like to start their reading at the end of books.

So, if you want to create a climate where:	then it will go best if:
• excellent performance is robust, self-sustaining and self-improving; • individuals and groups act spontaneously and with good interpersonal skills to tackle any interactions which are less than optimal to the achievement of the organization's goals; • good working relationships enhance positive collective feelings about community and individual self-esteem and effectiveness.	• there is an organization-wide vision and a strategy for turning it into reality; • there are objectives down to unit level which are accepted and understood; • middle managers are convinced about the high status of their new influencing role; • there is strong senior manager commitment to supporting and reinforcing the process in high profile ways. See Chapter 2, 'Key Interactions'

If you want:	then it will go best if:
• a co-ordinated drive across the whole of the organization to deliver the organization-wide vision; • managers at all levels thinking strategically and planning to achieve sustainable competitive advantage for the organization and to maximize their unit's contribution to that end.	• there is an organization-wide vision and a leader with the will to make it happen; • there is a senior management group who believe in the vision and have the character and credibility to lead and manage it in; • there is a ccmpulsion to seize any competitive advantage for the organization as a whole and to maximize the contribution of its constituent parts to that end; • there is a conviction that strategic thinking at all levels has a positive contribution to make to the success of the organization. See 'Planning to Win' in Chapter 3

If you want:	then it will go best if:
• to win over the hearts and minds of that key group of people, the middle managers, so that they engage themselves fully in their new influencing role and are prepared to spend their time and energies backing the organization's journey toward healthier social capital.	• the senior managers are fully committed and are prepared to invest their own time and effort in the task; • a population of middle managers exists, many of whom have the potential to make a positive contribution, if only they can be engaged; • there exists in the minds of leader and senior managers a strong conviction that the middle managers' new influencing role is genuinely higher status and more powerful than the old controlling one; • there is a clear picture of what that role looks like in practice; • there is a willingness on the part of the organization to deal with people's negative feelings about change as legitimate; • there is a willingness to cut out real dead wood quickly; • there is a willingness on the part of leader and senior managers to stick their necks out and be role models of the new ways. See Chapter 4 'Hearts and Minds'

If you want:	then it will go best if:
• your first-line managers and some of their key people – opinion formers and the like – delivering the goods in ways which are both highly efficient and consistent with the development of healthier social capital; • to free up your managers to carry out higher quality work and increase their span of responsibility; • to achieve significant improvements in performance along with cost savings.	• middle managers are at one with their new role, even if they have not yet mastered all of its intricacies; • middle managers carry a conviction that their people must be developed and that this is a central part of their role; • there is a determination in leader and senior managers to support a challenging training and development programme through to a successful conclusion and the personal stamina to bring that about; • there is a belief that training and development initiatives so far have just not produced the positive impact expected. See Chapter 5 on 'Delivering the Goods'

If you want:	then you can:
• to get the most out of your people and have them feel good about themselves, each other and the organization in the process; • to maximize productivity, reduce costs and excel in the delivery of performance measures and bottom line results.	• use any of these six processes anytime, but if they are to have maximum impact and produce the best return on the investment, then the role of coach and facilitator must be seen as more than some kind of touchy-feely add-on to the real work; • there must also be a willingness to allow people to behave as adults. This means both demanding that they take responsibility and allowing them the freedom to use it. See Chapter 6, 'Tapping the Geyser'

If you want:	then it will go best if:
• people who are capable and willing to generate new and potentially unique ideas for products, services, systems, and ways of working; • an environment which facilitates and contributes to people's ability to 'think out of the box' and encourages the application of winning ideas.	• the leader champions creativity and innovation, and reference to it is included in the organization-wide vision; • senior managers recognize that creativity and innovation is an effective way of working for everyone in the organization, irrespective of their function or position; • middle and first-line managers and other key influencers feel comfortable with the idea of creativity and innovation, see them as just 'the way we do things here' and change as an opportunity. See Chapter 7, 'And now for something completely different'.

References

Adams, Douglas (1979) *Hitch-Hikers Guide to the Galaxy – Life, the Universe and Everything*, Pan.

Amabile, Theresa (1999) *How to Kill Creativity*, Harvard Business Review on Breakthrough Thinking, HBS Press.

Coleman, James, S. (1988) Social Capital in the Creation of Human Capital, *American Journal of Sociology*, 94, 85–120.

Fukuyama, Francis (1995) *Trust – The Social Virtues and the Creation of Prosperity*, Penguin Economics.

Fukuyama, Francis (1999) *The Great Disruption, Human Nature and the Reconstitution of Social Order*, Profile books.

Goleman, Daniel (2000) Leadership that Gets Results, *Harvard Business Review*, 78(2), 78–90.

Goleman, Daniel (1995) *Emotional Intelligence*, Bantam.

Goleman, Daniel (1998) *Working with Emotional Intelligence*, Bantam.

Gould, Stephen Jay (1989) *Wonderful Life, The Burgess Shale and the Nature of History*, Penguin.

Honey and Mumford (1992) *Manual of Learning Styles and Learning Style Questionnaire*, Peter Honey.

McGill, Ian and Beatty, Liz (1992) *Action Learning*, Kogan Page.

Revans, Reg (1983) *The ABC of Action Learning*, Chartwell-Bratt.

Index

Activator 28, 111
  role definition 10
  training and development 111–32
  engaging 111–32
  checklist 116–17
  checklist 122–4
Adult behaviour and relationships 93,
  100–1
Altruism reciprocal 15–18
Attracting and retaining the best people
  27, 62, 121, 188, 191

Belonging – a sense of 12, 27, 34–6, 63,
  65, 90, 112, 115, 120, 165, 168, 187,
  190, 193, 196
Bloodshot eye 52, *see* Key Interactions

Candy store training and development
  116
Challenge statement 68–9
Coaching 44, 49, 60, 82, 84, 88, 90,
  95–6, 106, 119, 120, 124, 130, 134
  role in developing social capital
  135–9
  fields of freedom 25, 101–2, 109, 125,
  127
  checklist 142
Coherence, momentum and relevance
  112–14, 121
Collective effectiveness 35, 40, 43, 65,
  139, 167, 189

Combining 171, 181
Commitment to the greater good 12, 17,
  27–8, 33, 58, 63, 104, 112, 122, 139,
  151, 156, 191
Commonality of purpose 21, 27, 58, 65,
  67, 112, 114, 151, 189
Commonwealth 21, 36, 67, 158, 189,
  190
Communication strategy 104–7, 178
Community 2, 11, 33–5, 63, 65, 67, 84,
  121, 159, 170, 186, 188
  of interest 26, 34, 65, 134, 158,
  193
Competence 16–17
Competition 20–2, 36–8
Competitive advantage 172, 179
  sustainable competitive advantage
  62–3
  sustainable value-add 62–3
  SWOT analysis for SCA and SV-a
  70–2
Conflict handling 156
Confronting 156
  checklist 158–9
Contracting 43, 48–9, 140, 142–9
  a real example 144–6
  the principles of 146–7
  the practical steps 147–9
  checklist 150
Control versus influence 88, 91, 95, 137,
  191

Controls – minimising cost of 17, 40, 93
Co-operation 20–2, 34–6
Core Managers 28, 50, 82, 113, 130
  role definition 10
  cast of players 82
  potential contribution 82–4
  identifying and tackling the potential
    barriers 84–8
  introducing the new role 93–6
  engaging in social capital – eight
    actions 93–107
  engaging in training and development
    112, 125, 130
  checklist 91–3
  checklist 107–109
  checklist 109–110
Corporate village 187–189
Creativity 24–6, 121, 165–82, 171
  Uccello Process™ 151, 175, 178
  Process and steps 178–82
  cycle of organizational creativity and
    innovation 171–8
  checklist 182–4
Critical mass 45, 90, 111–13, 115, 118,
  120, 178
Cycle of organizational creativity and
  innovation 171–8

Daydreaming 66
Dialogues not monologues 104–7
Disciples 67, 75, 178
Douglas Adams 133, 146

E-mails, the web 189
Emotional Intelligence 58
Engaging
  Activators 111–31
  Core managers in social capital –
    eight actions 93–107
  Core managers in training and
    development 112, 125, 130
  people 60, 79, 81, 95, 100, 112, 134,
    152, 190

Facilitating 43, 50, 82, 90, 95–6,
  139–42
  masters of process 140, 160–2

learning sets 119, 133, 141, 159–62
checklist 142
Fields of Freedom 25, 101–2, 109, 125,
  127
Flight Crew role definition 9, 28, 52, 53
Francis Fukuyama 13, 31, 42, 57
Freeing up managers 122, 137

Generating ideas 72, 176

Hearts and minds 26, 58, 59, 107, 113,
  119, 122, 170, 178, 191
Heroes 22–4, 28
Hierarchy 81, 84

Influence versus control 88, 91, 95, 137,
  191
Innovation 25, 75, 165–82, 171
  cycle of organizational creativity and
    innovation 171–4
  checklist 182–4
Interactions 25–7, 33, 36, 37, 142, 157,
  165
  Key 31–56
  definition 40
  description of steps 42–51
  practitioner guide for introducing
    Key Interactions 51–6, 124
Interdependencies 65, 169, 170, 189
Investment 1, 5, 84, 102, 105, 111, 112,
  115, 118, 119
  return on 6, 33, 38, 41, 95, 100, 113,
    114, 115, 117, 118, 120–1, 123, 133,
    137, 143, 152, 162, 173, 187, 189,
    191

Key Interactions 31–56
  definition 40
  description of steps 42–51
  practitioner guide for introducing
    Key Interactions 51–6, 124
  checklist 40–2
  checklist 46–7

Labelling 86–7, 106, 147, 152
Leader, see Navigator
Leadership behaviour 57–8, 60, 90

heroes 22–4, 28
role model 20, 50, 60, 80, 96–8, 106, 159–60
positive behaviours 174
Learning 47, 100, 121
Learning on real work tasks 113, 118
practical applications 119, 121, 129
Learning sets 119, 133, 141, 159–62
checklist 162–3
Long hours culture 14, 188
Low maintenance, high performance 17, 40, 93
Loyalty 25–7, 134, 190, 191

Management by walking about 97
Managerial behaviour 57–8, 60
Managing expectations 96
Market deals 13–14, 15–18, 40, 43, 50
checklist 151–5
Marketing 62, focus on SCA and SV-a 73–5
Maximising the utilisation of resources 27, 134, 139, 159
Middle managers 80, see Core managers
Modular training and development for Activators
the argument for 111–14
a real example 114–16
the principal programme features 117–22
return on investment 115
for the organization 120–1
for the people 121
pitfalls 121
Core manager contribution 118
Flight Crew contribution 119
evaluation 120 and 131–2
the essential detail for practitioners 124–32
programme champion 124
steering group 125–6
shape and flow 127–8
Module defined 117–18
workshops 118

Navigator role definition 8, 28, 59

Negotiating market deals 15–18, 40, 43, 48–9
five stages 151–4
checklist 155–6

Parent/child relationships 100
Partisan victories 62, 112, 121, 139, 140, 153, 156
checklist 142
Performance 17, 27, 32, 37, 39, 43, 60, 93, 107, 114, 117, 121, 122, 123, 132, 143, 154, 162, 166, 168, 170, 179, 189, 190
low maintenance, high performance 17, 40, 93
Physical environment
bricks and mortar, steel and plastic 186–7
corporate village 187–9
Planning Groups 60
the role 67–9, 73
Planning to Win 60, 61
the process in outline 64–5
the process stage by stage 65–76
marketing 62
focus on SCA and SV-a 73–5
Policies, actual and declared 24–5, 98, 103
Presenteeism, long hours culture 14, 188
Progress, excitement and involvement 118, 120, 121, 169

Reciprocal altruism 15–18
Recognition 44, 50, 60, 85, 96, 99
Reinforcement 19, 60, 93, 98–9, 118, 120
Reliability 13–15
Reputation 18–20, 35, 65, 151
Restructuring 189
Return on investment 6, 33, 38, 41, 95, 100, 113, 114, 115, 117, 118, 120–1, 123, 133, 137, 143, 152, 162, 173, 187, 189, 191
Risk taking 24–5, 120, 126, 160, 169, 175
Robert Townsend 57, 187

Robust, self-sustaining and self-improving 40, 114, 134, 190
Role definition
Navigator 8, 28, 60
Flight Crew 9, 28
Core Manager 10
Activator 10
Role model 20, 51, 60, 80, 96–7, 106
positive behaviours 174

Self-image 18–20, 35, 85
Self-interest 2, 20, 31, 36–7, 42, 63, 83, 90, 104, 134, 165, 168–9, 194
Senior managers, *see* Navigator and Role definitions
Signals 98–9, 125, 130, 187
Slartibartfast 146, 151
SMART application plans 125, 127, 130, 154, 162
Social capital 24, 32, 37, 43, 57, 58, 60, 63, 65, 67, 73, 76, 79, 82, 83, 90, 91, 97, 101, 102, 104, 111, 114, 117, 120, 122, 134, 135, 140, 143, 151, 156, 159, 165, 177, 178, 186, 187, 190, 190
checklist 17–18
checklist 29–30
Social capitalists 157
Society 1, 5, 20, 27, 32, 167, 169, 191
Strategic planning
Planning to Win 60, 61
the process in outline 64–5
the process stage by stage 65
sustainable competitive advantage 61–2
sustainable value-add 61–3
SWOT analysis for SCA and SV-a 69–72
planning groups 60
the role of planning groups 66–70, 73
checklist 61
checklist 76–7
Strategic thinking 58, 61, 65, 91, 120, 191
Strategy devising a 72–5
Support 47, 50, 101, 116, 121
for Activator programme 118

personal 118–120
system 120
functions 63
Sustainable Competitive Advantage 61–2
Sustainable Value-add 61–3
SWOT analysis for SCA and SV-a 69–70

Tactical positioning guide 122, 193–6
Tapping the talent 60, 139, 159, 168
Teambuilding 36, 38–9
Teams 115, 191
Terms and conditions 190
Three-dimensional people 13, 14, 162
Total Quality Management 112, 166
Training and development
of Activators 111–32
candy store 112, 116
engaging Core managers in 112, 125, 130
Transactional analysis 100
parent/child relationships 100
adult behaviour and relationships 93, 100–1
Trust 2, 13–15, 20–2, 39, 65, 101, 103, 115

Uccello® Process 153, 175, 177
process and steps 178–82
checklist 182–4
United Distillers and Vintners 114–16, 120

Value statements 14, 68
Vision – defining and developing 65–6
Vision story 66, 68
Visionary 28, 80
Visions from inspiration to reality 58–9, 80

Win/win 62, 153, 154
partisan victories 62, 112, 121, 139, 140, 153, 156
checklist 142
Winning ideas 62, 179